ENGLISH PROFICIENCY:
Developing Your Reading
and
Writing Power

ENGLISH PROFICIENCY:
Developing Your Reading
and
Writing Power

RICHARD M. BOSSONE

and
Research Foundation/City University of New York

Research Assistants and Contributors
Grace Conley   Amy Ehrlich   Lora Kahn

McGraw-Hill Book Company
New York   St. Louis   San Francisco   Dallas   Atlanta

Special Acknowledgments

The author and publishers are indebted to the many students who participated in the research study that formed the basis of this program and whose paragraphs and essays have been adapted as models in the text.

Editorial Development: John A. Rothermich
Editing and Styling: Alma Graham
                              Naomi Russell
Design: Joe Nicholosi
              Margaret Amirassefi
Production: Angela Kardovich

Consulting Editor: Louise Baer

Library of Congress Cataloging in Publication Data
Bossone, Richard M., date
   English proficiency.

   Includes index.
   1. Exposition (Rhetoric) 2. English
language—Composition and exercises. 3. English
language—Grammar—1950–   I. New York (City).
City University of New York.   Research Foundation.
II. Title.
PE1429.B55   808'.042   78-14528
ISBN 0-07-006591-8

CONTENTS

SECTION 1:
READING AND WRITING ESSAYS

v

SECTION 2:
GUIDE TO REVISING PAPERS

SECTION 3:
HANDBOOK

INTRODUCTION

    This book will teach you how to read and write expository essays. Why is reading and writing this type of essay important? Most courses in school and many jobs require you to read for information and understanding. Most courses in school also require you to organize your ideas and present them effectively to your teachers and classmates. College placement tests often include the reading and the writing of an expository essay. In addition, by learning to write such essays, you will be able to handle almost any writing situation that requires you to organize your thoughts. Finally, and most importantly, learning to write is learning to think more clearly, no matter what the occasion. The ability to recognize logical thinking in what you read and to use such thinking is essential in your school, business, and personal life.

    In this book, reading and writing will be taught together. Why? Because by improving your reading, you will improve your writing. When you discover how authors put their works together, you will be able to use this knowledge in your own writing. The reverse is also true. When your own writing improves and you learn how to compose an expository essay, you will find it easier to read and understand someone else's essay.

SECTION 1: READING AND WRITING ESSAYS

UNIT ONE:

An Overview:
FINDING OUT WHAT YOU KNOW ABOUT READING AND WRITING AN ESSAY

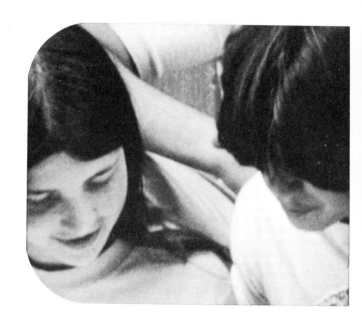

This unit is designed to help you find out what you already know about reading and writing essays. If you decide that you are going to take swimming lessons, your coach will first work with you to discover how much skill you already have. Are you a "beginner," an "intermediate," or an "advanced" swimmer? By finding out beforehand just how much you know and how much skill you have, you and your coach can concentrate on the skills you need especially to work on.

In this unit, then, you will test yourself to see what skill you already have in reading and writing essays. You will also get an overview of what the whole book is about. When you have finished the unit, you will have a good idea of what you are expected to learn and what units and lessons in the course you will need to work on most.

First, you will learn how each part of the essay contributes to the structure of the whole. Think of your plan for writing as being similar to an architect's design, or blueprint, for a house. Working from your plan, you first decide on a *controlling idea* (thesis statement). This is like laying the foundation of a house. Next, you

2

write logically by formulating *topic sentences*. These sentences are built on the controlling idea just as the wooden frame of a house is built on the foundation. Finally, you write the rest of the essay by giving *supporting details*. This completes your work, just as builders lay bricks and put up walls to complete a house.

Remember, being a good writer is not a talent with which you are born. Every good writer has had to work hard to succeed. But, with work, you will succeed!

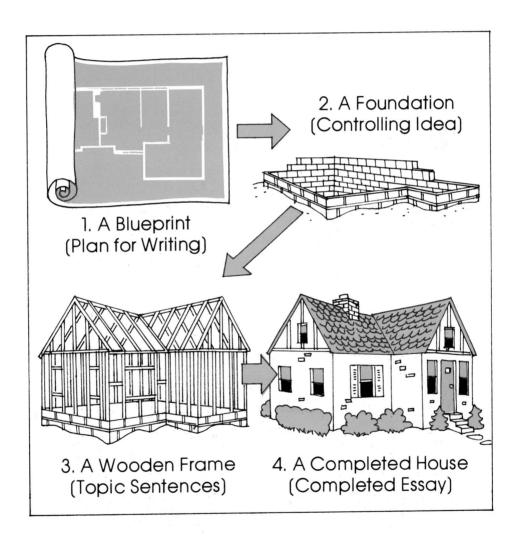

1. A Blueprint (Plan for Writing)

2. A Foundation (Controlling Idea)

3. A Wooden Frame (Topic Sentences)

4. A Completed House (Completed Essay)

Important Terms Used in This Book

1. Expository—a type of writing in which authors primarily use explanation to set forth their ideas.

2. Essay—a short, nonfictional prose composition on a single subject; sometimes called a *theme*.

3. Title—the name given to a composition. The title of an essay should give the reader an idea about the limited subject matter of the essay.

4. Introductory Paragraph—the first paragraph of an essay. The opening paragraph of an essay uses an introductory technique to gain the reader's attention and presents the controlling idea (thesis statement) of the essay.

5. Controlling Idea—the main idea that an author will develop in an essay. The controlling idea is expressed in a single sentence that should always be in the introductory paragraph; also known as *thesis statement*.

6. Body Paragraph—any paragraph that provides support for the controlling idea or thesis statement of an essay; also known as a *developmental paragraph*.

7. Topic Sentence—the sentence that tells what a body paragraph is about. The first sentence of a paragraph is usually the topic sentence.

8. Supporting-detail Sentences—sentences that back up, or support, the idea presented in a topic sentence. A topic sentence and supporting-detail sentences make up a body paragraph.

9. Concluding Paragraph—the final paragraph of an essay. The concluding paragraph of an essay uses some type of concluding technique to summarize and restate the controlling idea (thesis statement) of the essay.

4

Lesson 1

ANALYZING
THE FOUR-PARAGRAPH ESSAY:
TRANSFERRING FROM READING TO WRITING

LOOKING AHEAD

In This Lesson:

READ:

- to understand the overall organization of a four-paragraph essay.

- to analyze the various components of an essay in order to transfer this knowledge to your own writing.

WRITE:

- a four-paragraph expository essay.

Activity 1   Analyzing the Four-Paragraph Essay

You are probably wondering if you read as well as you should. This activity will help you to determine how well you read. Here is a model of an expository essay. Read it thoughtfully and carefully.

Problems of Cities and Suburbs

The city and the suburbs once seemed very different places. A city meant tall buildings, honking taxis, and smog-filled skies. The suburbs, on the other hand, meant family homes, gardens and lawns, and clean air. The problems faced by cities and suburbs also seemed quite different. Nowadays, however, *metropolitan* and suburban areas share many of the same problems, such as crime and drug addiction.

Crime is one problem found in both urban and suburban areas. Elderly people are mugged whether they are hurrying along a city street or strolling down a suburban avenue. Residents living in cities and suburbs hide in fear behind double-locked doors, hoping to prevent robberies. In both the cities and the suburbs, big, *vicious* dogs are used as additional protection against robberies. Even *juvenile* crime is a growing problem as gangs increase in the metropolitan and suburban areas.

Drug addiction is another problem shared by cities and suburbs. Young people growing up in overcrowded, unpleasant conditions in the city ghettoes often turn to drugs such as heroin for a temporary escape from life. Suburban youngsters turn to drug addiction to search for "kicks" and to put excitement into their boring lives. Often they become addicted to another kind of drug—alcohol. Whether the drug is heroin, cocaine, or alcohol, it can be bought quite easily either in a city or on a suburban school playground. Parents and officials in both areas are worried by the *prevalence* of drug addiction.

The "urban crisis," no longer limited to our cities, touches everyone. Even though our American cities and suburbs may still look different from each other, many problems facing these two areas today are really the same.

Exercise 1   Define the following words by seeing how they are used in the essay.

1. *metropolitan*—as used in paragraph 1. Pick out the word that means the same as *metropolitan:*
   - a. suburban
   - b. urban
   - c. rural

2. *vicious*—as used in paragraph 2. Pick out the word that means the same as *vicious:*
   - a. fierce
   - b. guard
   - c. frightening

3. *juvenile*—as used in paragraph 2. Pick out the word that means the same as *juvenile:*
  a. immature
  b. adult
  c. youth

4. *prevalence*—as used in paragraph 3. Pick out the word that means the same as *prevalence:*
  a. power
  b. widespread nature
  c. dangers

Exercise 2   Answer the following questions:

1. What is the title of this essay? _____

2. How many paragraphs are there? _____

3. Can you pick out from the following the one sentence in this essay that is the controlling idea (thesis statement)?
  a. Nowadays, however, metropolitan and suburban areas share many of the same problems, such as crime and drug addiction.
  b. Drug addiction is another problem shared by cities and suburbs.
  c. The "urban crisis," no longer limited to our cities, touches everyone.
  d. The problems faced by cities and suburbs also seemed quite different.

4. In the second paragraph (body or developmental paragraph 1), can you choose from the following one sentence that states the main idea of the paragraph?
  a. Even juvenile crime is a growing problem as gangs increase in the metropolitan and suburban areas.
  b. Elderly people are mugged whether they are hurrying along a city street or strolling down a suburban avenue.
  c. Crime is one problem found in both urban and suburban areas.
  d. In both the cities and the suburbs, big, vicious dogs are used as additional protection against robberies.
  e. Residents living in cities and suburbs hide in fear behind double-locked doors, hoping to prevent robberies.

5. In the third paragraph (body or developmental paragraph 2), can you choose from the following one sentence that states the main idea of the paragraph?

    a. Parents and officials in both areas are worried by the prevalence of drug addiction.

    b. Drug addiction is another problem shared by cities and suburbs.

    c. Whether the drug is heroin, cocaine, or alcohol, it can be bought quite easily either in a city or on a suburban school playground.

    d. Suburban youngsters turn to drug addiction to search for "kicks" and to put excitement into their boring lives.

6. Which sentence in the concluding paragraph best sums up that paragraph (and the whole essay)?

    a. The "urban crisis," no longer limited to our cities, touches everyone.

    b. Even though our American cities and suburbs may still look different from each other, many problems facing these two areas are really the same.

7. Is there any sentence in the concluding paragraph that is related to the introductory paragraph?

8. Who among the following might have written this essay?

    a. someone who lives in the city

    b. someone who lives in the suburbs

    c. someone from a foreign country

    d. someone who is familiar with the problems of cities and suburbs

Activity 2   Further Analysis of the Various Parts of the Four-Paragraph Essay

    This activity will show you a model structure of an essay—the main elements that hold up the finished project. It is important for you to understand this structure so that you can reproduce it in your own writing. Using this structure carefully will help you to organize an essay.

Model: If one were to visualize what a four-paragraph essay would look like, it might look like the drawing on the next page:

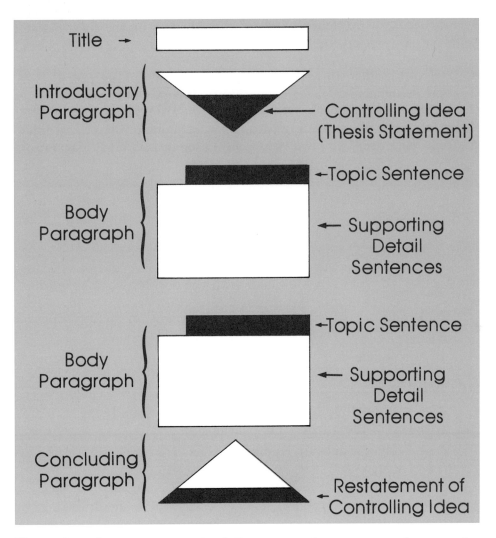

Exercise 1   Arrange the following in the correct order: conclusion, introductory paragraph, body paragraph 2, title, body paragraph 1.

1. _____

2. _____

3. _____

4. _____

5. _____

Exercise 2   Matching: Indicate which item on the right belongs
with which item on the left.

1. controlling idea (thesis statement)   a. body paragraph 1
2. topic sentence 1   b. body paragraph 2
3. subject of the essay   c. title
4. restatement of controlling idea   d. concluding paragraph
5. topic sentence 2   e. introductory paragraph

1. _____   2. _____   3. _____

4. _____   5. _____

Exercise 3   Fill in the blank with the correct word or words.

1. A _____ _____ (thesis statement) in the introductory
paragraph tells you what the entire essay is about.

2. A sentence that tells you what a body paragraph is about is

called a _____ sentence.

3. The controlling idea (thesis statement) is usually the _____
sentence in the introductory paragraph.

4. A body paragraph is made up of one topic sentence plus

_____ _____ sentences.

5. In a four-paragraph expository essay, there should be _____
topic sentences.

Activity 3   Writing a Four-Paragraph Expository Essay

As you read the following essay, note how it illustrates the principles of good organization. It has an introductory paragraph with a
controlling idea; two body paragraphs, each with a topic sentence
and supporting-detail sentences; and a concluding paragraph that
restates the controlling idea.

Handling Teenage Problems

Adults often say the teen years are the best. Most teenagers would probably disagree. Young people sometimes wish they could "go to sleep" for ten years and wake up in their twenties. The reason for this desire is that many teenagers feel swamped by the problems confronting them. Bodies growing and changing cause physical difficulties. Worries about school grades and careers cause mental anguish. And fears about finding a boyfriend or girlfriend cause emotional problems. It is much healthier, however, to deal with these problems instead of wishing to "sleep" them off. Two basic ways of handling teenage problems are to face and attack them directly or to work on them indirectly.

The easiest way to handle teenage problems is to attack them directly. Leroy, for example, feels his parents treat him like a baby. Whenever he tries to talk to them about this, he gets mad and starts shouting. To solve this problem, Leroy should face his parents directly, stop yelling, and talk sensibly to them. Most likely, his parents will soon see that he is behaving in a mature manner, and the problem will be solved. Selina, another teenager in the neighborhood, has just moved in and doesn't know anybody. Being lonely is no fun, and she wishes she had friends. If Selina attacks her problem head-on and becomes active in an organization, such as an athletic team, a glee club, a civic group, a school club, or student government, she will meet a lot of people and will probably make many new friends.

Sometimes teenagers can best handle problems indirectly. For example, sixteen-year-old Jody, at 5' 10", is much taller than her classmates. Self-conscious about this difference, Jody wears flat shoes, and she slouches to hide her height. Of course, Jody cannot handle her problem directly by becoming shorter, but she can work on her problem indirectly. Since many of the current fashions are designed for tall women, Jody should accent her height by wearing the high-styled fashions that shorter girls cannot wear gracefully. If Jody looked around her, she would realize that the focus today is on tall women and that many of her classmates are wearing platform shoes to appear taller. Jody should stand up straight and be proud of her long frame. She might even find her difference is her greatest physical asset. Fred has another problem. He dreams of becoming a doctor and works hard in school to accomplish this dream. But although Fred gets high marks in English, history, and foreign languages, he never gets 85s or 90s in mathematics and the sciences, the courses he needs to get into medical school. If Fred tries to attack his problem directly by studying even harder, he might have a nervous breakdown. Instead, Fred should concentrate on those subjects in which he excels and should redirect his goals so that he can use his talents in another challenging profession.

Because it is never easy to solve problems, finding a solution requires determination and common sense. In most instances, facing and attacking problems either directly or indirectly will solve most teenage troubles. Cheer up. Being a teenager lasts only seven years!

Exercise 1   Now let's see how well you can write a four-paragraph essay. Think of yourself or someone you know who has problems. Then write an essay on how you or that person handled his or her problem.

Remember, you must have:

1. an introductory paragraph with a controlling idea

2. two body paragraphs, each with a topic sentence and supporting-detail sentences

3. a concluding paragraph that restates the controlling idea

SUMMARY

In this lesson, you have read two model essays. These essays introduced you to the types of four-paragraph expository essays that you will read and write. You have also seen that the essay *structure* begins with a title, is followed by an introductory paragraph and two body (or developmental) paragraphs, and ends with a concluding paragraph. The purpose of this structure is to give both the writer and the reader a sense of organization. Only when you have organized your thoughts into this kind of logical pattern can you begin to write well.

UNIT TWO:

The Body Paragraph–
MINI-ESSAY

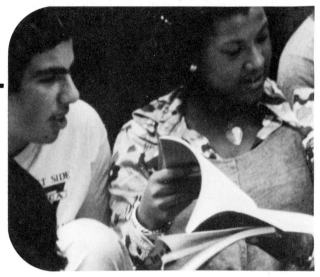

In Unit One, we compared writing an essay to building a house. A plan for writing is like a blueprint; a controlling idea is like a foundation; topic sentences are like wooden frames; and the completed essay is like the completed house. Writers use words as builders use bricks. Words and sentences have to be placed in certain patterns, just as bricks do. In this unit, we are going to see how sentences placed in certain patterns build body paragraphs.

A body paragraph is made up of sentences that center around a topic sentence and develop one thought. The writer uses a body paragraph to support an essay's controlling idea.

The body paragraph is really a mini-essay. It has a main idea (stated in the topic sentence) and a plan of organization. Also, like the essay, the body paragraph must have *unity* (must stick to one idea) and *coherence* (must develop that idea in a logical way). By learning to write effective body paragraphs, you will be learning the basic skills you will use in writing essays. *Remember:* When written on the page, the paragraph is similar to a punctuation mark. It is set up to indicate that it has been organized into a unit of thought. Therefore, when you begin a paragraph, indent the first line about an inch when writing and five spaces when typing.

Lesson 1
The Topic Sentence

LOOKING AHEAD

In This Lesson:

READ:

- to analyze topic sentences at the beginning of paragraphs and to see the effect of misplaced topic sentences in various positions in the paragraph.

WRITE:

- topic sentences, placing them at the beginning of the paragraph.

Activity 1   Reading and Analyzing Topic Sentences

What does a topic sentence do? The topic sentence states an idea that all the other sentences in the body (or developmental) paragraph support in some way. Never confuse a topic sentence with the controlling idea. The controlling idea is stated in the introductory paragraph and determines the content of the *entire* essay.

A topic sentence states the main idea of a *single* paragraph. As a beginning writer, you should place the topic sentence at the beginning of the paragraph. This will help you plan what you are going to say. If the main idea of the paragraph is stated in the first sentence, all the supporting details, reasons, or examples will naturally follow. Each of the following two paragraphs illustrates this plan of organization.

Eighteen-year-olds are worthy of the voting privilege because they have proven themselves responsible in a number of ways. Many eighteen-year-olds serve in our armed forces, head households, hold jobs, and pay taxes. Others are in college, successfully preparing themselves for future careers. While it is true that some eighteen-year-olds are immature and reckless, most in this age group are responsible and serious. The privilege of voting should continue to be given to eighteen-year-olds.

Topic Sentence

Eighteen-year-olds are worthy of the voting privilege because they have proven themselves responsible in a number of ways.

Number of Ways Eighteen-year-olds Are Responsible

serve in armed forces
head households
hold jobs
pay taxes
prepare for future careers

Marijuana, or "pot," is not a narcotic, but it still has some dangers of its own. Although marijuana does not produce addiction, as narcotics do, it can make the marijuana user psychologically dependent on it. Instead of coping with everyday problems, the marijuana user may withdraw through frequent use of the drug. Another danger of marijuana is that it can release inhibitions at inappropriate times. Any foreign substance introduced into the body is not without dangers, and marijuana is no exception.

Topic Sentence

Marijuana, or "pot," is not a narcotic, but it still has some dangers of its own.

The Dangers of Marijuana

makes user psychologically
  dependent
user may withdraw from everyday
  problems
can release inhibitions at
  inappropriate times

Here is a developmental paragraph in which the topic sentence is misplaced. Can you see why the underlined sentence should be the first one in the paragraph?

During the depression in the 1930s, people flocked to extravagant musicals, such as Busby Berkeley's *Gold Diggers of 1933*. People needed to be entertained in order to forget their gloomy, cheerless lives. Movies give us an escape to another world. During the recent unemployment of the 1970s, people flocked to disaster films like *The Poseidon Adventure* and *The Towering Inferno*. These exciting, if improbable, films provided a sure way to forget more immediate but less dramatic problems.

—Adapted from Ron Johnson and June Bone, *Understanding the Film*.

You can see that the topic sentence, "Movies give us an escape to another world," is the most important one in the paragraph. The supporting-detail sentences give the names of specific *movies* and give *reasons* why people needed to escape to another world.

MOVIES	REASONS PEOPLE NEEDED TO ESCAPE
1. *Gold Diggers of 1933*	**1.** depression of the thirties—to forget gloomy, cheerless lives.
2. *The Poseidon Adventure* *The Towering Inferno*	**2.** unemployment of the seventies—to forget more immediate problems

Exercise 1   The topic sentence of each of the following paragraphs is out of place. Find the topic sentence from among the other sentences of the paragraph and underline it. The first one is done for you.

1.   For instance, at the time of the great earthquake in Messina, Italy, in 1908, a pet cat felt the tremors, alerted the household with loud cries, and led the family to safety. Some cats have saved families from fire by crying out and warning their sleeping owners. Other cats have saved humans from poisonous snakes by attacking the reptiles before they could strike. <u>While we do not usually associate cats with acts of heroism toward human beings, there are recorded cases in which cats have saved people from injury or death.</u> In these and other acts of heroism, cats have shown that they are highly intelligent and capable of devotion to human beings.

—Adapted from J. J. McCoy, *The Complete Book of Cat Health and Care*.

2.   Astronauts will need food to eat, water to drink, and air to breathe. Among the problems facing future space travelers will be the problem of life support. Airless, waterless, and foodless outer space will not provide for these needs. The essentials for life will have to be carried aboard the spacecraft, or some method will have to be devised for manufacturing them on board.

—Adapted from *Science World*.

3. Earth people tend to be "down to earth," that is, matter of fact, conservative, careful. Water people are changeable, sometimes weak-willed. Air people are mercurial, communicative. According to astrology, the twelve signs of the zodiac, and the people born under each sign, are ruled by one or another of the four elements—earth, air, fire, and water. Fire people are ardent and *jovial*—a word, by the way, that derives from the influence of Jupiter.

—Adapted from *The New York Times Magazine*.

Activity 2 Writing Topic Sentences

Now it is your turn to try your hand at writing topic sentences. Topic sentences are signposts for a reader. They tell the reader what the paragraph is going to discuss.

Exercise 1   Read each set of facts listed below. Then think of an appropriate topic sentence that sums up all the facts that are given.

Example: Subway trains are fast.
            Subway trains get terribly crowded during rush hour.
            The noise on subway trains gets deafening sometimes.
            Subway trains often have the wrong destination listed.

Topic Sentence: Although subway trains are speedy, they present
                many annoying problems.

1. Many people won't leave their homes on Friday the thirteenth.
   Lots of buildings don't have a thirteenth floor.
   People don't like to walk under ladders.
   Some people believe that a black cat crossing their path means trouble.

   Topic Sentence: _____

2. Now that Lyle is attending a private school, he is not allowed to wear jeans.
   Blue blazers are required dress in Academy X.
   Diane will have to leave her platform shoes behind when she enrolls in a private school.
   Transferring out of a public school means no more dashikis for Jamar.

   Topic Sentence: _____

3. Shoplifters like to wear layers of clothing to disguise stolen merchandise.
Suitcases are handy places for hiding little objects.
Some people drop small pieces of jewelry under hats worn for that purpose.
One shoplifter even put something in a baby's diaper!

Topic Sentence: _____

SUMMARY

The topic sentence states the main idea of a body (developmental) paragraph. All the other sentences in the paragraph support the statement made in the topic sentence, which is usually the first sentence of the paragraph. Remember, the topic sentence tells the reader what the rest of the paragraph is going to be about.

Lesson 2

Structuring the Body Paragraph

LOOKING AHEAD

In This Lesson:

READ:

- to see how body paragraphs use supporting-detail sentences to develop the main idea stated in the topic sentence.
- to learn what kinds of details the supporting sentences may include.
- to familiarize yourself with three basic ways to organize paragraphs.

WRITE:

- a topic sentence in the form of a question that cannot be answered with a simple "yes" or "no."
- answers to the question asked by the topic sentence.
- a body paragraph with supporting-detail sentences that use facts, examples, or reasons which are organized by time order, comparison-contrast, or cause and effect.

You now know that the body, or developmental, paragraph of the expository essay *develops* the main idea stated in the topic sentence. "But," you may ask, "exactly *how* does it do this?" To understand how it does, think of the topic sentence as a question and the supporting-detail sentences as answers to that question. A good topic sentence should get a reaction from the reader. "Prove it to me." "Tell me why you think so." "Tell me how it can be done." "Give me more information to back up your claim."

For example, let us say your class has discussed an article entitled "Why Johnny Can't Write." The class has talked over the reasons given in the article telling why students' writing ability has declined over the last ten years. The homework assignment is to write an essay with the title "Why Today's Students Can't Write."

You decide to blame the decline of students' writing skills on television viewing and educational standards. The topic sentence of your first body paragraph may read like this:

Television has had a harmful effect on
the writing ability of America's students.

The rest of the paragraph would prove the truth of that claim. You would do this by changing the statement into a question in your mind and by answering that question.

Why has television had a harmful effect
on students' ability to write?

You give these reasons:

1. Time spent watching television is time that might otherwise be devoted to reading, an activity that will assist students in writing.

2. Children accustomed to passively watching television have difficulty with the active skills that reading and writing require.

3. Children trained on television viewing expect to be entertained in the classroom instead of taking an active role in their learning.

The topic sentence, together with the supporting-detail sentences, would read like this: (Notice that some qualifying words and a quotation have been added to give more force to the reasons.)

Many educators believe that television has had a harmful effect on the writing ability of American students. When they come to school, children accustomed to passively watching television have difficulty with the active skills that reading and writing require. These children have been trained to sit in front of the television screen. They expect to be entertained. Most of them have difficulty in doing things for themselves and taking an active role in their own learning. E. B. White, the well-known writer, agrees with the experts. "Short of throwing away all the television sets," he declares, "I don't know what we can do about writing."

Activity 1 Steps in Writing Effective Body Paragraphs

Consider the following steps when you begin to write a paragraph:

1. Turn the topic sentence into a question that cannot be answered with a "yes" or "no." For example, start the question by asking *how, why,* or *to what extent.*

2. List the answers to your question.

3. Evaluate each item on the basis of whether it does or does not answer the topic-sentence question. Even if the item does not answer the question of the topic sentence, you may still be able to use it if you put it into different words. "Television is entertaining" is not a good answer to the topic sentence of the model paragraph above. But "Television provides an easier kind of entertainment than the reading that leads to good writing" is a sentence that might be worked into the paragraph.

4. Rewrite the items on your list into logical, smooth-flowing sentences.

Exercise 1 Most of the following topic sentences will make good questions that will lead to effective supporting-detail sentences. Others will not. Change each of the statements into questions beginning with *how, why, to what extent,* or *in what way.* Write your question on the line below the statement. If you feel that you have enough knowledge to answer the question effectively, put an X in the box next to the sentence number. The first question is done for you.

☒ **1.** Final exams should be optional for students who have received good grades all semester.

Why should final exams be optional for students who have received good grades all semester?

☐ **2.** Snakes can be interesting once you get to know them.

_____

☐ **3.** Angie Dickinson is a good actress.

_____

☐ **4.** Popularity in school is more important than grades.

_____

☐ **5.** Roses are red.

_____

☐ **6.** Solar energy will be an important source of fuel in the future.

_____

☐ **7.** Teenage marriages are a good idea.

_____

Exercise 2   Now select two effective topic sentences that you turned into questions in Exercise 1 and write answers (supporting-detail sentences) for them.

1. Question: _____

Answers: _____

_____

_____

_____

_____

2. Question: _____

Answers: _____

_____

_____

_____

_____

Activity 2 The Supporting-Detail Sentences and What They Include

We have suggested that you think of the topic sentence as a question to be answered. The other sentences in the paragraph provide the answers to that question. However, they do more than merely answer the question. They also expand the reader's understanding of the subject under discussion. These sentences are called *supporting-detail sentences*. They support the topic sentence—that is, they give information that *proves* the topic sentence to be true and that makes the subject more interesting to read about. *Supporting* implies that every sentence "holds up" or "supports" the topic sentence in some way. *Detail* suggests that each sentence should note examples, names, and facts that will make your paragraph come alive.

As a beginning writer, you may find it helpful to think of your readers as individuals very much like you. They like to read about other people. They have emotions like yours and the senses of sight, taste, touch, smell, and hearing, just as you do. Thus, when you write, you will want to appeal to your readers' feelings and senses. You will want to involve them in the experiences of other people.

Nouns, adjectives, and numbers are categories of supporting details that create reader interest.

1. **NOUNS**
   Use names of real people, places, things.

   Mary Ann Kuwalkski . . . my best friend *Joe* . . . *Mrs. Harper* . . . *Indianapolis, Indiana*. . . . the Siamese *cat*. . . . her antique *chair*. . . . *The Greasy Spoon Restaurant*.

2. **ADJECTIVES**
   Use descriptive adjectives that bring your nouns to life.

   the *imaginative* fantasy, *Lord of the Rings*. . . . *the golden-haired pop* singer, John Denver. . . . a *crackling* blaze. . . . a *tender, butter-soft* piece of turkey on *whole wheat* bread.

3. **NUMBERS**
   Use statistics and numerical facts when your essay demands it.

   1862. . . . in *30* days. . . . *18* percent. . . . *30 000* people. . . . 7 billion dollars.

Exercise 1   For each paragraph, list the topic sentence and the details that the writer has used to support it.

Today, educators, psychologists, and social scientists are studying, more than ever, the impact of television on young people. A. C. Nielsen, a television survey-taker, reports that children under five watch an average of 23.5 hours of TV a week. Further, statistics show that by the time of high school graduation, the average student has put in a minimum of 15 000 hours before the screen, being exposed to 350 000 commercials and 18 000 killings. Evidence from 2300 studies and reports indicates that, other than parents, television is the most potent influence on the behavior of young people. And, unfortunately, the influence of television is all too often negative.

Topic sentence: _____

_____

_____

Details: _____

_____

_____

_____

_____

_____

_____

_____

_____

_____

_____

_____

_____

_____

_____

_____

It is a lengthy process to prepare chicle. Chicle, the ingredient that makes chewing gum chewy, comes from the sapodilla tree, which grows in Florida and other places with hot, steamy climates. Workers called *chicleros* cut zigzag slashes in the bark and gather the milky sap in bags. Each tree can be tapped only once every five years. At the factory, first the sap is boiled. Next, it is mixed with other substances. For example, it can be mixed with waxes, resins, and even rubber latex if it is to become bubble gum. Then, it is processed and pressed into a twenty-inch-wide continuous ribbon, ready to be cut, wrapped, sold, and chewed.

Topic sentence: _____

_____

_____

Details: _____

_____

_____

_____

_____

_____

_____

_____

_____

_____

_____

_____

_____

_____

_____

_____

_____

_____

_____

Exercise 2   Choose one of the following topic sentences to use in writing a paragraph. Before you begin writing, list the details in the column on the right.

Students have more problems than teachers realize.

Topic: *Student problems*

Details:

_____

_____

_____

_____

_____

_____

_____

_____

Thanksgiving is usually a time when many favorite American foods are served.

Topic: *Thanksgiving foods*

Details:

_____

_____

_____

_____

_____

_____

_____

_____

Activity 3 Types of Supporting-Detail Sentences

Supporting-detail sentences can take the form of facts, examples, or reasons.

The following paragraph develops the topic sentence through the use of *facts*, primarily numbers.

> Recreation has expanded greatly and has become more cultural in the last fifty years. In 1900, there were ten symphony orchestras in the United States; now there are 1200. Today, there are also more than 1500 local theatre groups, most of them amateur. People now spend more than $500 million annually on concert tickets. In 1934, 500 records of Beethoven's Ninth Symphony were bought; in 1954, 75 000. Twenty million of us play the piano, four million the guitar, and three million the violin. There are also two million Sunday painters.
> —Adapted from Bruce Bliven, "Using Your Leisure Is No Easy Task."

This paragraph gives *examples* of three different kinds of book owners, primarily by using nouns and adjectives.

> There are three kinds of book owners. The first has all the standard sets and bestsellers—unread, untouched. This deluded individual owns woodpulp and ink, not books. The second has a great many books—a few of them read through, most of them dipped into, but all of them as clean and shiny as the day they were bought. This person would probably like to make books her or his own but is restrained by a false respect for their physical appearance. The third has a few books or many—every one of them dog-eared and dilapidated, shaken and loosened by continual use, marked and scribbled in from front to back. This reader owns books.
> —Adapted from Mortimer J. Ader, "How to Mark a Book."

This paragraph develops the topic sentence by giving *reasons* in the supporting-detail sentences.

> We read fiction for several reasons. Most importantly, a book must be entertaining. Whether it is *Murder on the Orient Express* or *War and Peace*, it must be fun to read. Otherwise, only English teachers and literary critics would bother with it. Many of us seek escape in a book. Bored by our own lives or burdened by worries, we like to leave our narrow world and enter an imaginary one. There we can identify with characters whose lives are more exciting than ours and whose experiences we can never hope to have. Although we do not read fiction primarily for ideas,

we do discover insights in books which help us to understand human nature better. Good novelists know life. By reading their books, we broaden our own experience.

Exercise 1   Look back at the last paragraph you wrote for this course (page 26). Then answer the following questions based on that paragraph.

a. What concrete details and examples have you used in your supporting-detail sentences?

_____

b. What categories of details (nouns, adjectives, numbers) did you use?

_____

c. What are the types of supporting-details (reasons, examples, facts) that you used? Name some of them. _____

_____

d. What additional comments do you want to make about your paragraph?

_____

Exercise 2   Rewrite your paragraph, making sure it is filled with good supporting-detail sentences. If you wish, you can write a new paragraph. Remember to think of your topic sentence as a question that needs to be answered.

Activity 4 **Paragraph Patterns**

Almost everyone has seen the advertisement that proclaims (in large black type) "I was a 90-pound weakling." The ad tells how the sad young man pictured was ridiculed by his friends, rejected by his favorite girl, and humiliated at the beach, where he had sand thrown in his face. Then he enrolled in Mr. Hercules's weight-lifting course and turned his life around. As a muscle man, he defeats his sand-throwing enemy, attracts hordes of girls, and gains happiness forever after.

This young man's story can be used to illustrate three major paragraph patterns: (1) time order, (2) comparison-contrast, (3) cause and effect.

The *time-order pattern* relates a course of events that happen over a period of time. The time involved can be a minute, a day, or billions of years. In the 90-pound weakling's story, several incidents happened to enforce his feelings of inferiority. Then he took the "miraculous" body-building course and good things began happening to him. This story could be plotted on a time line.

favorite girl rejects him	*sand thrown in face*	*decision to take Mr. Hercules's course*	*victorious fight with enemy*	*attracts hordes of girls*

The *comparison-contrast pattern* does just what it says: it reveals how two things can be similar when they are *compared* or different when they are *contrasted*. In the young man's case, we have a definite contrast between his former skinny physique and his present powerful one.

The *cause-and-effect pattern* is equally clear in this story. The young man's misery *caused* him to enroll in the weight-lifting course. The *effect*, or result, of the course was his new and powerful body.

Exercise 1   The following three body paragraphs illustrate the three paragraph patterns we have been discussing: time order (or process), comparison-contrast, and cause and effect.

Read the first paragraph to find four crucial *times* mentioned. Put them on the time line provided. Look for "clue" words such as *then, next, after.*

Paragraph 1

Writing a good essay in class requires a sense of time and organization. During the first ten minutes, you must limit your subject and decide on a controlling idea. Then, in the next ten minutes, you should develop the controlling idea and write two topic sentences for your body paragraphs that follow logically from your controlling idea. These topic sentences should make two distinct points about your subject. The next twenty minutes should be spent writing the rest of the essay. You must write an introduction that includes your controlling idea. After this, you need to write supporting-detail sentences, logically arranged, to back up the topic sentences of the two body paragraphs. Having done all this, you need to develop a strong conclusion. Finally, during the remaining ten minutes, you must engage in proofreading and editing. All this is not easy, because clear writing is clear thinking that demands discipline and organization.

___/_____/_____/_____/___

Paragraph Pattern _____

In this second paragraph, there is a *contrast* provided between two types of students. In the boxes provided, indicate the two types that are being contrasted. Look for "clue" expressions such as *on the one hand . . . on the other hand, one . . . the other.*

Paragraph 2

There are mainly two types of students in high school: the serious students and the fun-loving students. The serious students are the academic types, usually quiet and reserved and always concerned about progressing in school. For a serious student, getting a good grade on a chemistry test is more important than getting a big hello from the kids in the class. The fun-loving students, on the other hand, are more involved with social activities and are more concerned about their popularity ratings. When these two types of students arrive at school, the serious students generally worry about a quiz, while the fun-loving students generally worry about their friends' reactions. Where one type of student conscientiously takes notes on what the teacher is saying, the other writes notes to pass to friends. Every high school has its share of these two types of students to lend variety to its campus.

Paragraph Pattern

Read this third paragraph to discover three *causes* and three *effects*. Indicate the causes to the left of the arrows, and indicate the effects to the right. Look for "clue" words such as *cause, result, effect* (noun), *affect* (verb).

Paragraph 3

Because of the close relationship between teacher and student, students tend to take on the characteristics of the teacher. For example, an uninterested teacher who does not really care about students or their learning problems will soon cause the students to lose interest in the course. Then there is the teacher who may know the subject thoroughly but is unable to communicate this knowledge to the students. The result of such a teacher's efforts will be bored, frustrated students. On the other hand, teachers who love teaching, know their subjects, can communicate well, and are enthusiastic will generally have a positive effect on their students. Such teachers tend to make their

31

students enthusiastic about learning and often bring about greater student achievement. Given these examples, one can safely assume that teacher attitudes truly affect student behavior.

_____ → _____

_____ → _____

_____ → _____

Paragraph Pattern _____

Exercise 2   Here are three paragraphs with a time-order pattern. When you have finished reading each paragraph, indicate on the time line the four or five *times* given in the paragraph. The first one is done for you.

Paragraph A

The world's population is growing at an alarming rate. Scientists estimate that the total number of people on the planet Earth in 1 A.D. was only 300 million. The growth rate increased at a steady pace until 1750, when the total population was 791 million. Then, with the advent of the Industrial Revolution, the growth rate accelerated, so that by 1900, only 150 years later, the 791 million figure had more than doubled to 1650 million. Between 1900 and 1970, the population more than doubled again; in 1970, the world population was 3625 million. If the growth rate continues at the same speed, demographers predict that the population will double every 37 years. By the year 2170, perhaps 157 billion human beings will occupy our already overcrowded planet. Demographers have aptly named this accelerating growth rate the "population explosion."

(150 years later)

1AD	1750	1900	1970	2170
/	/	/	/	/

Paragraph B

Scientific experiments reveal that most people who are kept from sleeping show similar symptoms. The first night, these people do not seem very tired. They can read or study. However, they do experience an attack of drowsiness between 3 A.M. and 6 A.M. During the second night, they feel entirely different. Their eyes are dry, and they have trouble remaining awake even if they remain on their feet, walking around.

During the early morning hours, the desire for sleep is almost overwhelming. At this time, many experience double vision. By the third night, these subjects cannot sit down without falling asleep. If they are asked to perform the simple task of counting their pulse, they forget the numbers after fifteen or twenty. The experiment usually continues until the fourth day, when these subjects are as sleepy as they are ever likely to be.

—Adapted from Nathaniel Kleitman, *Sleep and Wakefulness.*

___/_____/_____/_____/

Paragraph C

Trying to maintain one's home without any help can be an exhausting affair. People who have trees near their homes know that autumn means leaves—piles and piles of leaves. Many long hours spent with a rake are needed to clear lawns and sidewalks of those red and golden "pests." Then, just as homeowners are recovering from autumn, winter comes with its own problems. All those delicate flakes of snow, looking so light and airy, become very heavy when one has to shovel what seems like tons of them. Spring generally gives tired homeowners a boost of energy to turn their houses upside down for a thorough spring-cleaning. A small rest from this exhausting experience ends when summer comes. Then, homeowners are kept busy putting up screen windows, digging out fans from the basement, and dragging hoses outside to water the lawn. Taking care of a home is a yearlong, exhausting business.

___/_____/_____/_____/

Exercise 3   Here are four paragraphs that develop a comparison or contrast pattern. When you have finished reading each paragraph, indicate the two items that are compared or contrasted. The first one is done for you.

Paragraph A

As far as the senses go, the world is not as it seems. Sight must be different in different kinds of animals because their sense organs do not have the same range. Take human beings and bees. Because the human eye reacts to light waves of only a certain length, humans fail to respond to the shorter and longer waves of the optical spectrum. The bee is not limited in this way—at least so far as the shorter waves go. The bee can see ultraviolet. It responds to the ultraviolet color of the flower it uses for nectar. If the flower were red, however, the bee would see it as black.

—Adapted from Niko Tinberger *et al.*, *Animal Behavior*.

In Paragraph A, *human sight* is contrasted with the *sight of bees.*

Paragraph B

Two psychologists, Patricia Self and Nancy Daton, demonstrated that mothers do treat a baby according to its sex. Five mothers were handed Adam, a six-month-old boy in blue overalls. Six others were handed six-month-old Beth in a pink dress. The mothers who had Beth called her "sweet." They often gave her a doll to play with. Two mothers claimed they could "just tell" Beth was a girl. They smiled at her more frequently than the mothers who had Adam smiled at him. However, the differences were in their minds. Beth and Adam were the same six-month-old baby boy.

—Adapted from Alice Lake," "Are We Born into Our Sex Roles or Programmed into Them?"

In Paragraph B, _____ is contrasted with _____ .

Paragraph C

There are good and bad ways to study. A good way would be to plan your study time long before an important test or exam. Then you would have enough time to look over all the material and ask about something that you did not understand. A bad way would be to leave everything until the night before the test. Then you probably would not be able to cover everything, and you would not have time to check on what you did not know. Another good way to study would be to find a quiet place to work. You need some place where there are no distractions so you can concentrate on your work. A bad way to study would be to have a place that is noisy, with the TV blaring, the telephone ringing, or children playing in the background. Another good way to study would be to put all personal problems out of your mind. A bad way to study would be to let your attention wander back and forth to your personal problems. Studying effectively demands absolute concentration.

In Paragraph C, _____ are contrasted with _____ .

Paragraph D

Both conservative and liberal politicians want to see a prosperous and well-run country, but they differ on the ways to reach such a goal. The conservative believes that business should be left alone and thinks that jobs will result from the competitive system. The liberal believes that the government should interfere to create some jobs. The conservative fears that higher taxes and inflation will result from government interference with business. The liberal believes the involvement of the government is necessary to ensure that the needs of the poor and the unemployed are met.

In Paragraph D, _____ is contrasted with _____.

Exercise 4   Here are three cause-and-effect paragraphs. When you have finished reading each paragraph, indicate on the lines provided at least three causes and three effects that the paragraph describes. The first one is done for you.

Paragraph A

Human activities are changing the earth's climate for several reasons. One researcher calls the effect of human activities "the human volcano." He has shown how artificial clouds from commercial smoke, jet exhaust, and city smog affect the weather. Pollution from Chicago, Illinois, and Gary, Indiana, causes snow to fall on Lake Michigan's eastern shore. This happens because iron particles attract ice crystals.

CAUSE	EFFECT
human activities	- - - - - change climate
artificial clouds	- - - - - affect weather
pollution from Chicago and Gary	- - - - - causes snow to fall on Lake Michigan's eastern shore

Paragraph B

In the 1860s, Louis Pasteur taught the French how to keep wine from souring. Pasteur showed that the yeasts which cause wine to sour are alive. As the yeasts fed on the wine, their digestion made the wines ferment. This proved, Pasteur reasoned, that chemical reactions caused the basic life processes. Therefore, interfering with the chemical reactions and killing the yeast by gentle heating protected the wine.

CAUSE   EFFECT

_____ - - - - - _____

_____ - - - - - _____

_____ - - - - - _____

_____ - - - - - _____

Paragraph C

Drug research has produced a striking example of artificially produced animal behavior. Animal scientist Peter Witt discovered that drugs cause spiders to produce strange, misshapen webs. The drugs act on the spiders very much as they act on humans. A stimulant-type drug caused the spider to be impatient and to spin on one small area. Chloral hydrate, which puts humans to sleep, also puts spiders to sleep, and their webs are left unfinished. Caffeine produced a haphazard tangle of threads as the spider exhibited "coffee nerves."

—Adapted from Niko Tinberger, *Animal Behavior*.

CAUSE   EFFECT

_____ - - - - - _____

_____ - - - - - _____

_____ - - - - - _____

Exercise 5   In this exercise, you will write body paragraphs in each of the three basic patterns.

1. Use specific details (nouns, adjectives, numbers) to write a body paragraph developed with a *time-order* pattern. Start with the topic sentence given, or write one of your own choosing.

    Experiences in my childhood taught me about the roles women and men were expected to play in this society.

    When you have completed your paragraph, fill out a time-line diagram for it.

2. Use specific details (nouns, adjectives, numbers) to write a body paragraph developed with a *comparison-contrast* pattern. Start with the topic sentence given, or write one of your own.

    In general, women are much _____ *than men.*
    (*you fill in*)

    When you have completed your paragraph, make a comparison-contrast diagram for it.

3. Use specific details (nouns, adjectives, numbers) to write a body paragraph developed with a *cause-and-effect* pattern. Start with the topic sentences given, or write one of your own.

    Male chauvinism causes problems for many women. (or) *Liberated women cause problems for many men.*

    When you have completed your paragraph, make a cause-and-effect diagram for it.

SUMMARY

In a body or developmental paragraph, the main idea is stated in the topic sentence and developed through supporting-detail sentences. These sentences can be made lively if you use nouns, adjectives, and numbers. Supporting-detail sentences can take the form of facts, examples, or reasons. The three major paragraph patterns are: time order, comparison-contrast, and cause and effect.

Lesson 3
Keeping the Main Idea in Mind

LOOKING AHEAD

In This Lesson:

READ:

- to analyze the way sentences are related to the topic sentence in order to develop unity.
- to note how effective arrangement of details and skillful use of linking words and transitions develop coherence in the paragraph.

WRITE:

- unified paragraphs with good topic sentences and properly related supporting-detail sentences.
- coherent paragraphs with effectively arranged details and skillfully used linking words and transitions.

Activity 1   Unity in the Paragraph

You already have some idea of what the word *unity* means. You have probably heard the saying "In unity there is strength." *Unity* means a joining together of many parts into a single whole. The whole is strong when the parts work together for the good of the whole. This is true in writing an essay or in painting a beautiful picture.

You can think of the topic sentence of your paragraph as an agreement with your reader. This agreement (the subject of the paragraph) is stated in the topic sentence. If all the sentences in the paragraph talk about that subject, we say that the paragraph has unity.

As you become more aware of effective writing techniques, you will notice that topic sentences do not always appear at the beginning of a paragraph. Sometimes you will find them at the end or even in the middle of a paragraph. But, until you are more experienced, it will be helpful to you if you place your topic sentence at the beginning of each body paragraph.

The following paragraph is unified under the topic "team spirit." Each of the sentences contributes to the idea of what team spirit is. As you read through the paragraph, make a mental note of the way each sentence adds to the idea stated in the topic sentence.

(1) Team spirit is essential to any cooperative effort. (2) Anyone who owns a business knows that workers will do better work if they like each other and if they believe in the goals of the company. (3) Any good coach will encourage his or her players to "go out there and play for the good of the team!" (4) There is such a thing as a home-team advantage because the cheering of the home-team fans inspires their team to play harder. (5) Team spirit can operate in the classroom also. (6) One teacher discovered that students worked better if everyone was seated in a circle instead of in the traditional rows with all the students facing the teacher. (7) The circular arrangement created a cooperative atmosphere and the impression that everyone had something to contribute. (8) Learning then became a team effort.

Now discover how each sentence contributes to the idea of team spirit.

The topic sentence is: "Team spirit is essential to any cooperative effort."

Sentence 2 describes team spirit in business with the words: "workers will do better work if they like each other and if they believe in the goals of the company."

Sentence 3 describes team spirit in sports with the words: "play for the good of the team!"

Sentence 4 again describes team spirit in sports, but this time the emphasis is on the fans, as is shown by the words: "the cheering of the home-team fans inspires their team to play harder."

Sentence 5 introduces the idea of team spirit in the classroom.

Sentence 6 tells how to make students feel part of a team, citing the example: "students worked better if everyone was seated in a circle."

Sentence 7 continues to define and describe team spirit in the classroom, pointing to "a cooperative atmosphere and the impression that everyone had something to contribute."

Sentence 8 sums up the ideas of sentences 5–7 with the words: "Learning then became a team effort."

Exercise 1   Each group of sentences below makes up a paragraph. All the sentences are in order except the topic sentence, which should be the first sentence of the paragraph. Find the topic sentence and put an X in the square next to it. The first one is done for you.

Paragraph A

- ☐ **1.** The ninth floor button was removed from the elevators that served the new high-rise addition.
- ☐ **2.** Only those with a key could take the elevators above the ninth floor.
- ☐ **3.** Directly facing the elevator door when one emerged on the penthouse level was an armed guard at a desk.
- ☐ **4.** Beyond the guard's desk, Hughes had a partition installed with a locked door.
- ☒ **5.** When Howard Hughes moved to the Desert Inn in 1966, he constructed elaborate precautions in his penthouse.
- ☐ **6.** His own guards, stationed a few yards away, never saw their employer in his four years at the Desert Inn.

Paragraph B

- ☐ **1.** Sexual love often means pleasure for oneself, without regard for the partner.
- ☐ **2.** True love should not be selfish in this manner.
- ☐ **3.** Too many adolescents do not realize that love means more than gratification of sexual desires.
- ☐ **4.** Instead, love should imply caring more for someone else than for yourself.
- ☐ **5.** The love that most religious leaders refer to fits this definition.

Paragraph C

☐ **1.** We no longer speak of poor people but of the *disadvantaged.*

☐ **2.** Too many of us in our everyday language drift toward fuzziness of speech.

☐ **3.** We do not ask where we are but where we are *at.*

☐ **4.** The edges of our moments blur into *time frames.*

☐ **5.** Some people never *say* anything; instead, they *indicate* something.

Exercise 2   A paragraph has unity if every sentence stays on the subject that is stated in the topic sentence.   Each of the following paragraphs has one sentence that does not belong with the others. Find the out-of-place sentence and put an X in the box next to it.   The first one is done for you.

Paragraph A

☐ **1.** In the 1950s, some teenagers were too concerned with superficial things.

☐ **2.** My friends and I worried about how to keep the pennies centered in our penny loafers and how to keep our "flip" hairstyles flipped.

☐ **3.** A major crisis was not having a date for the prom.

☐ **4.** A major disaster was not getting into the sorority or fraternity of one's choice.

☒ **5.** Such power seems to impress everyone except Henry Winkler.

Paragraph B

☐ **1.** Although students may not realize it, they have a lot in common with their teachers.

☐ **2.** On a beautiful spring day, teachers, like the pupils, would secretly prefer to be outside the classroom.

☐ **3.** My mother says spring is the best time of the year.

☐ **4.** Tired teachers and students both count the days until a long-awaited vacation begins.

☐ **5.** Having to mark tests and essays can be as big a job as taking the tests and writing the essays.

☐ **6.** A teacher who has to write an "F" on a paper can be almost as disappointed as the student who receives the grade.

☐ **7.** On the happier side, a teacher who writes an "A" on a paper can be as pleased as the hardworking student.

Paragraph C

☐ **1.** Jimmy Carter believes that the "state and pomp" of the modern presidency has gone too far.

☐ **2.** As the first farmer to run for president since Thomas Jefferson, he would like to return to Jefferson's simpler ways.

☐ **3.** Carter asked prominent Republicans to recommend candidates for cabinet posts.

☐ **4.** As Georgia's Chief Executive, he sometimes surprised visitors by appearing barefoot and in blue jeans.

☐ **5.** Carter's desire to send his daughter to public school in Washington was well received by the black population of the capital.

☐ **6.** His insistence on carrying his own luggage, however, brought him criticism from the press.

Exercise 3   Write a unified paragraph using *one* of these two topic sentences or a sentence of your own choosing.

1. One of the advantages of youth is being open to new experiences.

2. Young people sometimes suffer from the disadvantage of not being taken seriously by adults.

Remember, in a unified paragraph, each sentence must stay on the subject given in the topic sentence.

Activity 2   **Coherence in the Paragraph**

As we noted in the previous activity, paragraph *unity* refers to the way in which each sentence relates to the topic sentence.

Coherence refers to the ways in which each sentence relates to the other sentences in the paragraph.   Since the word *cohere* means "to stick together," a paragraph is coherent when the sentences follow one another naturally or when they are tied together by repeated key words or special linking words and transitions.

Coherence by Following a Natural Sentence Order

Some ideas are put together through a natural order that is built into the process. For example, let us say you want to bake a cake. Before you begin, you read the recipe. Then you check to see that you have all the ingredients. Next, you combine the ingredients in a specific order, put the cake into the oven, and wait a certain amount of time for the cake to bake. In other words, you proceed step by step, following a natural order.

Some paragraphs deal with subjects that follow a natural order. Read the paragraph below and note how the directions for growing an avocado plant are in a logical order and give coherence to the paragraph:

(1) An inexpensive way to add living things to your house is to root common kitchen seeds. (2) The avocado seed is particularly easy to grow. (3) First soak an avocado pit in water until the skin can be removed easily. (4) Then secure three toothpicks in the middle of the pit to balance it in a jar or glass of water. (5) Make sure that half of the seed (the pointed end) is out of the water and that the other half is submerged. (6) Water the plant approximately every three days so that the water in the jar remains at a constant level. (7) Keep the jar in a light but not too sunny location. (8) It will take a few weeks for the seed to split and sprout. (9) After a few days of sprouting, transplant the seed into a pot of earth or potting soil. (10) Then watch the sprouted seed grow into a beautiful avocado plant.

—Adapted from Sharon Cadwallader, *In Celebration of Small Things*

Note that each sentence in this paragraph carries the reader a little further along with directions for growing the plant.

Coherence by Repeated Key Words and Use of Pronouns

Not every paragraph has a natural sentence order. As a writer, you can use the device of repeated words to achieve coherence in your paragraphs. This means repeating a key word several times in your paragraph. Sometimes, several key words are repeated. In the example above, the important word *seed* is repeated in sentences 2, 5, 8, 9, and 10. The word *pit* is repeated in sentences 3 and 4; *grow* is repeated in sentences 2 and 10.

Repeating the exact word may get repetitious. If you wish to avoid needless repetition, you can use synonyms. Words that are synonyms are words that can mean approximately the same thing, depending on the context. For example, *plant* and *living thing* are synonyms as used in the paragraph above. *Soil* and *earth* are also synonyms. Can you find others?

Another way of achieving coherence without repeating exactly the same word is to use pronouns. Pronouns provide a welcome relief from the repetition of the same noun throughout the paragraph. In the example above, "it" in sentence 4 takes the place of "the pit."

Coherence by Linking Words

At other times in your writing, you will need to reply on linking words to show your reader the connection between your ideas. The English language contains many linking words. Some of the most common and useful ones are the following:

Linking Word	How Used	Example
also	to indicate addition or continuation	I enjoy the beach because I like to swim in the ocean. I *also* like to relax on the sand.
moreover	(other linking words of this type are *in addition, again, furthermore, first, second*)	If we use energy conservation techniques, we won't be dependent on oil from foreign countries. *Moreover*, we will save money on heating bills.
however	to show contrast	Paula loves sweet things, such as candy and bubble gum. *However*, her dentist recommended that she eat fewer sweets to prevent cavities.
nevertheless	(other linking words of this type are *notwithstanding, yet, on the other hand, still*)	Jordan thought *One Flew Over the Cuckoo's Nest* was a stimulating novel and play. *Nevertheless*, he disliked the movie version.
for instance	to give examples (other linking words of this type are *for example, as an illustration, in other words, that is, in particular*)	Sherry felt that she might make a good architect; *for instance*, she loved drawing plans and utilizing space well.

simi-larly	to show a likeness between things (other linking words of this type are *like-wise, in a like man-ner, in the same way, in a similar case*)	Many of the Romantic poets died when they were still young. John Keats did not reach his twenty-sixth birthday, and Percy Bysshe Shelley, *similarly*, died before he was thirty.
there-fore thus	to indicate results (other linking words of this type are *con-sequently, as a result, so, then, hence*)	Marlene hoped to be a flight at-tendant. *Therefore*, she studied for-eign languages. Poverty areas are often plagued with rats. *Thus*, many ghetto chil-dren die each year of rat bites.
indeed	to show emphasis (other linking words of this type are *in fact, certainly, truly, admittedly*)	Harriet is extremely talented in all sorts of crafts. *Indeed*, her favor-ite hobby is knitting.
finally	to summarize or con-clude (other linking words of this type are *to sum up, in conclu-sion, in summary, in short*)	If you follow the steps outlined above, you will write a good essay. *Finally*, remember to proofread what-ever you wrote before you hand it in.

Read the paragraph below and note how the linking words oper-ate in, and give coherence to, the paragraph:

Most dentists say that chewing gum is bad for your teeth. The sugar in the chewing gum grinds into the teeth and lodges in the crevices between the teeth. Therefore, the chances for tooth decay are greatly increased. As a result, we now have sugarless gum. So the problem of tooth decay from sugar in chewing gum can now be avoided. However, some dentists still advise their patients not to chew gum.

Exercise 1   Read the paragraph below carefully, noting the relationships among the sentences.   Then select the linking word to the
left of each blank that better expresses the link between one sentence
and another.

Items of clothing sometimes change as status symbols.

However	_____, furs have traditionally been status
For example	
Nevertheless	symbols. _____, with the growing concern
Similarly	for wildlife conservation, the wearing of certain furs has
Therefore	lost its prestige. _____, various groups within
Moreover	a society have different ideas about clothes as status

a society have different ideas about clothes as status
symbols.   Blue jeans, a traditional work garment, were
adopted as a nonstatus item for everyday wear in the
1960s by those who were protesting the fact that society
was too concerned with status and money.   Jeans were
low in cost and were so durable that they seldom needed

Indeed
However

replacing. _____, by the early seventies,
the age, degree of fadedness and wear, and fit of one's
jeans became a symbol of the wearer's status.

Nevertheless
Likewise

_____, though jeans were popularized in an
attempt to reduce the emphasis on money and status, one
can now buy jean outfits costing several hundred dollars.

Exercise 2   Read the following paragraph, noting how it is
coherent.

(1) In most cases of drug addiction, the drug addicts turn to drugs
because of a desire to escape from reality.   (2) They cannot cope with the
daily problems that most of us face.   (3) Indeed, the "high" from the drugs
clouds their minds and shields them from reality.   (4) Sometimes, however,
addicts lose touch with reality altogether and live in a world of illusion.
(5) Some drugs, LSD in particular, cause hallucinations that can be
pleasant but that can also be frightening.   (6) In fact, certain drugs take
addicts so far away from reality that the drugs can cause lasting mental
damage.

Exercise 3   Using the paragraph you just read, discuss the three ways the author achieved coherence: natural order, repeated words, and linking words.

For example—Sentence 3 includes a linking word (*indeed*), repeated key words (*drugs* and *reality*), and pronouns (*their* and *them*).

SUMMARY

Two qualities of good paragraphs are *unity* and *coherence*. *Unity* is achieved when each sentence stays on the subject stated in the topic sentence. *Coherence* is achieved by following a natural order, repeating key words, and using linking words.

UNIT THREE:

The Essay–
GETTING STARTED

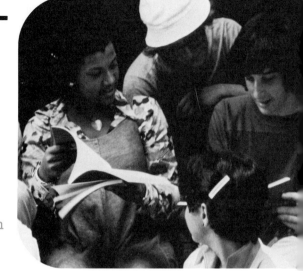

In this unit, you will begin work on the essay by thinking about what you must do before you write the whole essay.

Naturally, thinking *while* you are writing is crucial, but thinking *before* you begin to write is just as important. Most people neglect this step; as a result, their writing suffers.

What should you think about before actually beginning? You should think about the following:

1. what you are going to write about (choosing and limiting your subject);
2. how you will present your controlling idea (thesis statement);
3. what support you will provide for your controlling idea.

Although this may sound a bit overwhelming, these activities can be handled by carefully noting what follows. This unit will show you ways to choose and limit a subject so that it can be adequately treated in a four-paragraph essay. In addition, this unit will help you phrase a good strong sentence stating your controlling idea. Finally, this unit will help you in reading and writing various introductory and developmental paragraphs.

Lesson 1
Selecting a Subject

LOOKING AHEAD

In This Lesson:

READ:

- leading questions of a personal nature to stimulate thinking about yourself.
- newspaper headlines to develop ideas for writing.

WRITE:

- statements based on your personal experience.
- statements based on current events.

Activity 1 **Looking "Inside" to Find a Subject**

Obviously, before you begin writing an essay, you must have something to write about. In this book, you will usually be given general subjects to write on, similar to those most teachers give you. But what do you do if you must (or wish to) choose your own subject? How do you begin? The best method is to look within yourself.

Reading often helps you to look within yourself. Frequently, characters in a book you like give you some insight about yourself. Think about the personalities of characters that you admire, their motivations, and their dreams. Perhaps you like these characters because you see something of yourself in them.

Now read about the characters below. Maybe you will see yourself in one of them.

Student 1 loves to tinker with a car's engine and can take apart anything mechanical and put it together again.
Broad Topics Found From Looking "Inside":
1. How to Save Money with Do-It-Yourself Repairs
2. Cars and Their Engines
3. The Satisfaction of Working with Your Hands

Student 2 is a music fan, plays a tape deck all the time and is always among the first to know the latest dances.
Broad Topics Found From Looking "Inside":
1. Why Listening to Music Is Important
2. Differences between Rock Groups
3. Expressing Feelings through Dance

Student 3, the oldest of five children, has many difficulties in coping with such a large family.
Broad Topics Found From Looking "Inside":
1. The Good (or Bad) Points of Large Families
2. Problems of Being the Oldest
3. Sibling Rivalry

Student 4 is an eighteen-year-old student who does not have any special hobbies or interests.
Broad Topics Found From Looking "Inside":
1. Problems of Being a Teenager
2. Typical Teenagers: Do They Really Exist?
3. Eighteen-Year-Olds and the Vote

Exercise 1   Let's begin to look inside. Think about your past, your present, your hopes for the future. List—in time order—important events during your early childhood and your elementary and high school days. Now, using your list, write an essay about yourself.

Exercise 2   Think a little deeper about yourself—your home life, school life, love life, social life, religious or moral life. Ask yourself questions like this: How do I feel about my home life, my school life, my social life? Then translate your feelings into a general statement (a broad topic) such as one on the following page:

home life: Good Points about Apartment Living
school life: High School Should Not Be Mandatory

love life:	"Dating" Is Dead
social life:	Importance of Friends
religious life:	Putting Your Religion into Practice
parents:	Parents Were Teenagers, Too
brothers, sisters, and only children:	The Benefits of Being an Only Child
relatives:	Family Get-Togethers
home environment:	Reasons for Needing Privacy

Now list five broad topics you could write about—from looking inside yourself. You may use any one of the categories listed above on the left or other categories of your own choosing.

1. _____

2. _____

3. _____

4. _____

5. _____

Exercise 3   Read the following sentences and list three possible broad subjects that this student could write about—just from the information given here.

A seventeen-year-old high school student just got a driver's license. This teenager loves to drive but always gripes about the high insurance rates.

Three broad topics based on the information above are:

1. _____

2. _____

3. _____

Activity 2 Looking "Around" to Find a Subject

Besides writing about yourself, you can choose subjects that are of special interest to your readers, teachers, and classmates. Study the world around you and look for timely and important topics in the news: prominent people who are succeeding or failing, major events that will affect your readers, conflicts that exist between the sexes.

EXAMPLES OF HEADLINES FROM A NEWSPAPER
AND THE SUBJECTS THEY SUGGEST

HEADLINE	THREE BROAD SUBJECTS
Stiff Antidrug Laws Are No Deterrent	Tough Narcotics Laws Should Be Changed Better Ways to Stop Drug Addiction Reasons for Illegal Drug Use
Survey Finds Many Teenagers Are Ignorant about Government	Should "Government" Be Taught in School? Why Citizens Should Be Informed about the Government Ways to Learn about the Workings of Government
Cheating at West Point Causes Scandal	Rise in Cheating among Students Honor System Needs a Replacement Academic Pressure Can Cause Cheating

Exercise 1   Read your newspaper and note the headlines. Think about the important issues of the day. Then list three broad topics you could write about, possibly through doing some further reading.

1. _____

2. _____

3. _____

SUMMARY

Selecting a subject for your expository essay will not be a problem once you realize how many interesting subjects you are already capable of handling. Your family background, your hobbies and interests, your beliefs—all the things "inside" you can become broad subjects. International affairs, newspaper headlines, television newscasts, magazine articles—the world "around" you can also provide many broad subjects for writing.

Lesson 2
Limiting the Subject

LOOKING AHEAD

In This Lesson:

READ:

- examples that illustrate the process of limiting a subject.

WRITE:

- titles that illustrate limited subjects.

Once you have selected a broad subject, you must narrow it down, making it smaller and smaller. This will make the subject easier for you to handle and will also make the subject fit the limits of your assignments. (In this book, remember, you are mainly writing four-paragraph essays.) Writing about too broad a subject is like trying to park a big car in a small space. You can try all day, but you can never fit a large limousine into a small spot meant for a sports car.

Let's examine the subjects listed in the chart on the next page. *Religion* is a huge subject, and a four-paragraph essay simply cannot handle it adequately. Moreover, a slightly limited subject like "Differences between Judaism and Christianity" is not good, either. There are many major differences that could be mentioned—different views on the Messiah, different types of holidays and customs, different thoughts on sin. An entire book could be written on this slightly limited subject. An additional problem is that *Christianity*, itself, is too broad a term. Should Roman Catholic views be mentioned? What about the beliefs of the Protestant denominations? And is Greek Ortho-

BROAD SUBJECT	SLIGHTLY LIMITED	LIMITED
RELIGION	Differences between Judaism and Christianity	Lutheran and Jewish Beliefs about the Resurrection of the Dead
	Separation of Church and State in the United States	Prayer in Public School Classrooms
	Priests, Nuns, and Marriage	The Historical Explanation for a Celibate Catholic Clergy
	The New Popularity of Eastern Religions	Reasons for the New Popularity of Eastern Religions among Young People
	The Rise in "Born Again" Christians	The Political Advantages of Being a "Born Again" Christian

dox thinking to be included? This is why a limited subject is most suitable for a four-paragraph essay. In going from the *slightly limited* subject, "Differences between Judaism and Christianity," to a *limited* subject, "Lutheran and Jewish Beliefs about the Resurrection of the Dead," *Christianity* is limited to *Lutheran,* and only *one* difference is chosen to work with, the resurrection of the dead.

This diagram shows how you must progress from a broad subject to a slightly limited subject, to a truly limited subject.

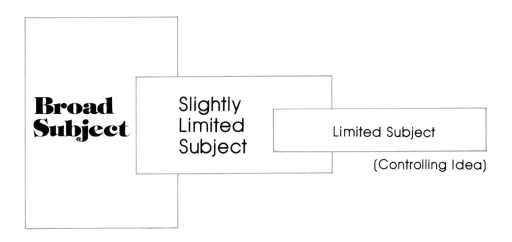

Broad Subject / Slightly Limited Subject / Limited Subject (Controlling Idea)

Activity 1 — Understanding the Process of Limiting a Subject

Let's say your general subject is English. Here is one of the many possibilities for limiting it.

Broad Subject:
English
Slightly Limited:
The Necessity of Studying English
Limited:
Studying English Is Necessary for Anyone Planning a Career in Business

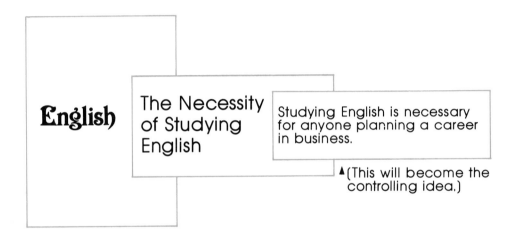

English | The Necessity of Studying English | Studying English is necessary for anyone planning a career in business.

▲(This will become the controlling idea.)

Exercise 1   This exercise deals with deciding whether a subject is limited or only slightly limited. First, read the broad subject on the left. Then look at the statements on the right. Next to each statement on the right, write "limited," if you think such is the case, or "slightly limited," if that is the case. The first one is done for you.

BROAD SUBJECT		STATEMENT
1. Horoscopes	**a.** *slightly limited*	Horoscopes and the Public
	b. *slightly limited*	Horoscopes in Far Eastern Cultures
	c. *limited*	Three Reasons for Believing in Horoscopes

2. Television   **a.** _____   Ways to Limit Violence on Television

                 b. _____   Violence on Television

                 c. _____   Violence on Television Encourages Violence on the Streets

3. Sports   **a.** _____   Athletes and Million-Dollar Salaries

                 b. _____   Two Athletes Who Are Worth $1 000 000

                 c. _____   Should an Athlete Earn More Money Than a Teacher?

4. Comic Strips   **a.** _____   Why *Peanuts* Is Realistic

                 b. _____   How Comic Strips Reflect Real Life

                 c. _____   Realism in Comic Strips

Exercise 2   In the following exercise, read the broad subject and note the slightly limited subjects below. Then write limited subjects for each topic. The first one is done for you.

1. The broad subject is *Gambling*.

     Slightly Limited Subjects: **a.** Legalization of Gambling
                                     b. Gambling and Churches

     Limited Subjects: **a.** Why Gambling Should Be Legalized in the United States
                                     b. Why Churches Should Not Have "Las Vegas Nights"

2. The broad subject is *Prejudice*.

     Slightly Limited Subjects: **a.** Fighting Prejudice
                                     b. Blacks and Unemployment

     Limited Subjects: **a.** _____

                                   b. _____

3. The broad subject is *Films*.

Slightly Limited Subjects: **a.** New Films and the Heroic Nonhero
b. Three-and-a-Half Dollar Admission Charges to Films

Limited Subjects: **a.** _____

_____

b. _____

_____

4. The broad subject is *Drugs*.

Slightly Limited Subjects: **a.** Cocaine—The New "In" Drug
b. Tranquilizers and Legal Drug Abuse

Limited Subjects: **a.** _____

_____

b. _____

_____

Activity 2 Continuing to Limit the Subject

Why are we spending so much time on limiting subjects? The answer is simple. Limiting a subject will make it easier for you to write a good controlling idea and a good essay.

Here is an example to show you the connection between limited subjects and controlling ideas:

A student wanted to write a four-paragraph essay on her favorite writer, William Shakespeare. She knew the subject was too broad, so she limited it to "The Plays of William Shakespeare." She wrote a controlling idea and an introductory paragraph using this subject, but she was not pleased. Then she went back and limited her subject still more, titling her essay: "Problems Found in Shakespeare's Plays Are Similar to Those of Today." She then wrote a new controlling idea for her introduction.

Here are her two introductory paragraphs. They are identical except for the last sentence in each—the first controlling idea and the rewritten one:

| 1 | 2 |
| Ask anyone involved with English literature "Who is the greatest writer?" and you will undoubtedly hear one name mentioned: William Shakespeare. Although this country boy who "made it" died 360 years ago, his thirty-seven plays are still valued and loved today. Why? Part of the answer is that Shakespeare was a genius, and his plays are masterpieces. | Ask anyone involved with English literature "Who is the greatest writer?" and you will undoubtedly hear one name mentioned: William Shakespeare. Although this country boy who "made it" died 360 years ago, his thirty-seven plays are still valued today. Why? Part of the answer is that Shakespeare dealt with issues that still concern us today, such as prejudice and parent-child problems. |

Exercise 1   Reread the two paragraphs above about Shakespeare. Then answer the following questions:

1. Which paragraph uses the controlling idea written from the more limited subject?

1 or 2

2. Which controlling idea sounds more specific and interesting?

1 or 2

Exercise 2   Here, the broad subject, *Television*, has been slightly limited. Now limit it still more.

> Broad Subject - - - - - - - - - - -   Television
> Slightly Limited Subject - - - -   Television Encourages Learning
>
> Limited Subject - - - - - - - - -   _____

The ability to see both sides of a question is important. Now write a limited subject taking the opposite point of view from the one you just wrote.

> Broad Subject - - - - - - - - - - -   Television
> Slightly Limited Subject - - - -   Television Discourages Learning
>
> Limited Subject - - - - - - - - -   _____

Exercise 3   Look "inside" your own experiences to find a broad subject, and work from there.

Examples of Broad Subjects: Living in the Suburbs (or Country or City)

High School Mathematics (or some other school subject)

Being a Baptist (or a member of some other religious group)

Broad Subject - - - - - - - - - - -   _____

Slightly Limited Subject - - - -   _____

Limited Subject - - - - - - - - -   _____

Now look "around" you (as in newspapers, newscasts, magazines, articles) to find a broad subject.

Examples of Broad Subjects: Birth Control

Arab-Israeli Conflict

IRA (Irish Republican Army) Bombings

Broad Subject - - - - - - - - - - -   _____

Slightly Limited Subject - - - -   _____

Limited Subject - - - - - - - - -   _____

SUMMARY

Many subjects that are too broad for a four-paragraph essay can be limited by concentrating on one aspect of the broad subject. Even then, subjects often have to be limited further to be treated adequately in a short essay. Try to move from a broad subject to a slightly limited subject to a limited subject.

Lesson 3
Stating the Controlling Idea
(Thesis Statement)

LOOKING AHEAD

In This Lesson:

READ:

- to understand what a controlling idea is by studying examples.
- to understand the three basic items contained in a good controlling idea.

WRITE:

- your own controlling ideas.

The key to writing a good essay is the controlling idea. The controlling idea is a one-sentence statement that contains a subject, a verb, and a key term that can be divided into different examples or aspects. These examples or aspects of the subject can then be developed in the body paragraphs.

Controlling idea is a better name for this important sentence than *thesis statement,* which is used in some books, because the word *control* suggests that this sentence is the powerful one upon which all other sentences depend. Here are some suggestions that may help you to formulate the controlling idea of your essay:

1. Make the subject your own. Be sure you know about the subject that you want to discuss or know where to find information on it. News articles and magazines are good sources for information on current subjects.

2. Develop an "image list" to help you get started on the subject you select. Write down all the "pictures" you can think of about your subject, using single words or phrases. From these pictures or images, an emerging thought will appear. The emerging thought will then help you to state a controlling idea.

3. Give yourself a purpose for writing. Ask yourself why the subject interests you and why you want to write about it. The answers to these questions will give you a "handle" on what you want to discuss. Then the particular slant you take on the subject will give your audience a reason for reading the essay.

4. Be sure your subject is narrow. The image list may help you to choose certain aspects of the subject. These aspects will become central to the controlling idea.

Activity 1   Using an "Image List"

To understand more fully how you might use the four suggestions for formulating a controlling idea, read what one student did:

Sharon was in training for the track team. She realized that she would have to change her eating habits if she wanted to perform well. She began to read the labels on the foods that she bought. She also read articles and listened to news reports on the artificial ingredients that were added to foods. When she was assigned an expository essay in English class, she decided to write on the food industry.

1. She read all she could find on the subject.

2. She developed an "image list" on the food industry and on food advertising.

   Image List on the Food Industry and on Food Advertising
   Greasy hamburgers

   Singing commercial: "Have it your way at Burger King."

   Catchy phrase: "At McDonald's, we do it all for you."

   Friendly Tony the Tiger: "It's g-r-r-reat"—sugarcoated cereals, cavities, bad for your teeth.

   "Kellogg's best for you" song; little nutritive value in cornflakes.

3. She decided that her purpose in writing the essay would be to discuss how the American public buys what is advertised rather than what is good and healthy to eat.

When Sharon looked over her image list, she saw a pattern emerging: advertisers are out to sell food that isn't good for us.

From this emerging thought, Sharon developed a controlling idea: *Television advertising encourages us by clever techniques to buy food that has little nutritive value.*

Note that this controlling idea is a sentence that has:

a subject: television advertising

a verb: encourages

a key term that
  can be divided: clever techniques (of advertising)

Exercise 1   Study the way one student approached writing about life in New York City:

Image List:	crowded subways	center of culture
	high rents	beautiful parks
	a great deal of crime	many colleges and universities
	dirty air	great restaurants

Emerging thought from images: Some images reflect what is good about life in New York City, and others reflect what is bad.

Controlling idea: Living in New York City involves both good and bad experiences.

a subject: living in New York City

a verb: involves

a key term that
  can be divided   experiences (good and bad)

Now continue with the exercise, filling in the blanks where necessary:

1. Subject: Being Old

   Image List: Grandmother can be rude if   loneliness
                 she wants to.

                 more likely to get mugged   death is closer

                 doesn't have to go to work or
                 school anymore

                 lots of knowledge through
                 experience

   Emerging thought from images: Being old involves advantages and disadvantages.

   Controlling idea:_____

                    a subject: _____

                    a verb: _____

                    a key term that can be divided: _____

2. Subject: Modern American Movie Heroes

   Image List: Robert Redford—good-looking, athletic, in control
                 Dustin Hoffman—not traditionally good-looking,
                 shy
                 Woody Allen—frail, insecure, a weakling
                 John Travolta—powerful, strong, masculine
                 Charles Bronson—a he-man, sure of himself

   Emerging thought from images: _____

   Controlling idea:_____

                    a subject: _____

                    a verb: _____

                    a key term that can be divided: _____

3. Subject: Trends in Rock Music (or Pop, Folk, or Jazz, if you prefer)

Image List: _____

Emerging thought from images: _____

Controlling idea: _____

        a subject: _____

        a verb: _____

        a key term that can be divided: _____

Activity 2 Comprehending the Function of Controlling Ideas

Your controlling idea should be focused on the one major idea of your paper. As noted above, there should be three items in your controlling idea:

1. a subject

2. a verb

3. a key term that can be divided

Let's look at some examples to help us understand further these three basic items:

1. The popularity of high school football has increased for several reasons.

a subject:	the popularity of high school football
a verb:	has increased
a key term that can be divided: (this will be divided into the different *reasons*)	for several reasons

2. The plots of the television serial *Mary Hartman, Mary Hartman* satirized aspects of daytime soap operas.

a subject:	the plots of the television serial *Mary Hartman, Mary Hartman*
a verb:	satirized (poked fun)
a key term that can be divided: (this will be divided into the different *aspects*)	aspects of daytime soap operas

Your controlling idea tells your reader what will be discussed in the rest of the essay. It should be a statement that you are able to defend, an opinion that you are willing to support.

Note also that the ways you can divide the "key term that can be divided" will eventually become subjects of the topic sentences in your two body paragraphs.

CAUTION! Your controlling idea should NOT be :

just a title, such as	The Decline of Baseball
just an announcement, such as	I would like to talk about my gym teacher.
just a statement of absolute fact, such as	Suicide means deliberately taking your own life.

Using what we have learned about having (1) a limited subject, (2) a verb, and (3) a key term that can be divided, let's rewrite the unsatisfactory controlling ideas noted above.

UNSATISFACTORY	GOOD
The Decline of Baseball	The decline of baseball affects many types of businesses.
I would like to talk about my gym teacher.	My gym teacher influenced me in several ways.
Suicide means deliberately taking your own life.	Suicide is on the rise for several reasons.

Note: There may be times in your reading when the controlling idea of an essay will not contain a key term that can be divided. Sometimes, an experienced author will simply *imply* such a term. For example, if you read, "A young teacher must strive to achieve discipline in the classroom," the term that can be divided is implied: A young teacher must strive to achieve discipline in the classroom *in many ways.* At other times, the points to be made in a piece of writing will be stated in the controlling idea. For example, the controlling idea of one essay might be stated as follows: Two basic ways of handling teenage problems are to face and attack them *directly* or to deal with them *indirectly.* Here, the two ways of handling teenage problems are specifically noted—to face and attack them directly or to deal with them indirectly.

Exercise 1   Read the controlling ideas written below. Then copy out the subject, verb, and key term that can be divided, just as we did in examples 1 and 2 on pages 65–66.

1. American society today embraces many kinds of life-styles.

a subject: _____

a verb:_____

a key term that can be divided: _____

2. Reading books can help people escape from reality in different ways.

a subject: _____

a verb:_____

a key term that can be divided: _____

3. The movie *Gone with the Wind* depicts aspects of life in the South a century ago.

a subject: _____

a verb:_____

a key term that can be divided: _____

4. All people find their own ways of achieving happiness.

a subject: _____

a verb:_____

a key term that can be divided: _____

Exercise 2   To make sure you understand a controlling idea, that is, a statement that you are willing to defend or support, read the following controlling ideas and answer the questions that follow. The first one is done for you.

1. Apple trees provide people with shade and fruit.
   a. What type of trees are mentioned here? *apple trees*
   b. According to the controlling idea, are these trees good or bad? *good*
   c. What do the trees provide? *shade and fruit*

2. In certain regions, wooden houses last longer and provide more insulation than brick houses.
   a. What are the two types of houses being compared?

   _____ __

   b. Which type is better? _____

   c. What are the reasons given? _____

3. Left-handed people are discriminated against in several ways.

   a. What people are being discussed? _____

   b. Does the author think "lefties" or "righties" have an

   easier time? _____

   c. In how many ways are left-handed people discriminated

   against? _____

4. School vacations give students a chance to relax or to earn money with a summer job.

   a. What type of vacation is mentioned here? _____

   b. Are vacations a waste of time or beneficial? _____

   c. What are the two things vacations give students? _____

   _____

Exercise 3   Read the following items to see if they are good controlling ideas. If you find a good controlling idea, put a check mark next to it.

_____ 1. Contact lenses are better than eyeglasses.

_____ 2. Contact lenses are better than eyeglasses in several important ways.

_____ 3. Scientists have two theories explaining why the sky is blue.

_____ 4. The sky is blue.

_____ 5. Cats are better pets than dogs because they are smarter.

_____ 6. Cat lovers have many reasons for preferring cats to dogs as pets.

Exercise 4   Read each statement below. Write *yes* next to the ones that would make good controlling ideas. Write *no* next to the ones that would not be good.

_____ 1. I would like to discuss why tax reform is necessary.

_____ 2. George Washington was our first President.

_____ 3. The decline in our birth rate.

_____ 4. Tax reform is necessary for many reasons.

_____ 5. TV programs center mainly on violence and sex.

Exercise 5   The five statements below do not make good controlling ideas. Rewrite each one so that it has a subject, a verb, and a key term that can be divided.

1. Spring is the most beautiful season.
2. Cigarette smoking is unhealthy.
3. I would like to prevent World War III.
4. Men should do more housework.
5. The government should rebuild our city.

Exercise 6   Read the following two introductory paragraphs, paying special attention to the controlling ideas. After reading the introductory paragraphs, read the rest of the essay to find out which controlling idea really states the main idea of the entire essay.

Here are the two introductory paragraphs:

Hairstyles and Individuals

Paragraph A

Americans tend to be obsessed with hair. Hundreds of shampoos and conditioners, all promising miracles, are on the market. Blow dryers, brushes, and other equipment cost Americans thousands of dollars. And all this is just for hair. Yet hair is more than an attractive covering on our heads. In fact, *hairstyles supply a good deal of information about an individual.*

Paragraph B

Americans tend to be obsessed with hair. Hundreds of shampoos and conditioners, all promising miracles, are on the market. Blow dryers, brushes, and other equipment cost Americans thousands of dollars. And all this is just for hair. Yet hair is more than an attractive covering on our heads. In fact, *hairstyles are quite interesting.*

Now read the rest of the essay and answer this question: Which controlling idea—from Paragraph A or Paragraph B—really states the main idea of the entire essay?

A person's political beliefs can influence a choice of hairdo. The rock musical of the 1960s, *Hair,* showed this clearly. Shoulder-length locks on a young man meant that he was opposed to the Vietnam War, while a ponytail was a pretty sure sign that its owner was a "hippie." One's attitude toward the whole youth movement, with all its liberal political thinking, was revealed by the length of one's hair. On the other hand, if you saw a man with a crew cut, you could be fairly certain that he was political conservative. H. R. Haldeman, of Watergate fame, may be an example of the connection between political thinking and hairstyle. When Haldeman was a hard-line conservative type ("My country, right or wrong"), he had a crew cut. When he went to southern California to live, he let his hair grow longer.

Hairstyles can also reveal a person's cultural or religious beliefs. When the Black Movement became widely accepted, many blacks let their hair grow into an Afro. This hairdo proclaimed to the world: "I am black and I'm proud of it. I'm not going to force my hair into white styles

anymore, just as I'm going to have my own culture, not the white culture."
Most men who belong to the Hare Krishna movement shave their heads,
leaving only a long lock in the center. This hair is kept long to allow
their god to pull it and yank the wearer back onto the true path, if he has
strayed. Orthodox Jewish women must cover their hair, and the men must
keep curled earlocks to fulfill a religious commandment.

Studying somebody's hairstyle can be fascinating. You may even
find out some interesting information about the person, simply by glancing
at the hairdo. Now, what about Kojak?

Activity 3   Writing Controlling Ideas (Thesis Statements) by Working from Limited Subjects

Up until now, you have been reading and examining controlling
ideas that other people wrote. Perhaps you said to yourself, "I can do
that." Maybe you even said, "Some of these aren't too good. I bet I
can write better controlling ideas." Well, now is your chance. Remember to limit your subject *before* you write the controlling idea.

Exercise 1   Write a controlling idea for each of the following:

1. Broad Subject: Dreams

   Slightly Limited Subject: Interpreting Dreams

   Limited Subject: Common Symbols in Dreams

   Controlling Idea: _____

2. Broad Subject: Violence on TV

   Slightly Limited Subject: Effects of TV Violence on Children

   Limited Subject: Violence in *Starsky and Hutch* and Its Effect on
   Children

   Controlling Idea: _____

3. Broad Subject: Cars

   Slightly Limited Subject: Hobbies Involving Cars

   Limited Subject: Fun Hobbies: Stock Car Racing and Repairing
   Old Engines

   Controlling Idea: _____

Exercise 2   From the following list of subjects, choose two, limit them, and then write controlling ideas.

Broad Subjects: Politics

Religion

Art

Science

Education

Entertainment

Occupations

1. Broad Subject: _____

Slightly Limited: _____

Limited: _____

Controlling Idea: _____

2. Broad Subject: _____

Slightly Limited: _____

Limited: _____

Controlling Idea: _____

SUMMARY

A good controlling idea is probably the single most important item in a four-paragraph expository essay. This tells your reader what you think about a particular subject and what you are going to discuss in the body of your essay. A controlling idea should always include a subject, a verb, and a key term that can be divided.

Lesson 4

Writing Topic Sentences for the Controlling Idea

LOOKING AHEAD

In This Lesson:

READ:

- model topic sentences to understand how they follow logically from the controlling idea.

WRITE:

- topic sentences based on the controlling idea.

In Unit Two, you began to learn about topic sentences. Here, we will not only review what we covered there but will also see how topic sentences are developed from the controlling idea. In that unit, you learned that the controlling idea should contain a subject, a verb, and a key term that can be divided.

For example, one controlling idea may be as follows:

The book *Down These Mean Streets* by Peri Thomas depicts causes for ghetto problems.

a subject:	the book *Down These Mean Streets*
a verb:	depicts
a key term that can be divided:	causes for ghetto problems

Now divide the "key term that can be divided" into two different kinds of causes for the ghetto's problems—social and economic causes, for example. Then turn these causes into topic sentences:

Topic Sentence 1 (for body paragraph 1):
According to Piri Thomas, one of the causes for the problems of the ghetto is the social stigma of not being white.

Topic Sentence 2 (for body paragraph 2):
Another cause for ghetto problems examined in *Down These Mean Streets* is economic discrimination.

Activity 1 Reading and Analyzing Topic Sentences

Here you will do two exercises that will help establish the relationship between the controlling idea and the topic sentences.

Exercise 1   Read the following controlling ideas and topic sentences. Be prepared to explain how the topic sentences are derived from the controlling idea.

1. Controlling Idea—Every day, the citizens of big cities across the country face serious problems.

   Topic Sentence 1—Air pollution is one of the major problems in cities all over the country.

   Topic Sentence 2—The rise in crime is another serious problem with which urban citizens must contend.

2. Controlling Idea—Many men in the United States do not feel free to do certain things.

   Topic Sentence 1—One thing men have been taught not to do is to express emotions in public.

   Topic Sentence 2—Also, many men do not feel free to take jobs that have been traditionally held by women.

3. Controlling Idea—For men and for women, cologne remains the ideal gift for several reasons.

Topic Sentence 1—You don't have to know someone's size or color preferences in order to buy cologne.

Topic Sentence 2—Cologne is a personal gift, and yet it is not too intimate.

Exercise 2

Select from each list of topic sentences the two sentences that logically follow each controlling idea:

1. Controlling Idea: Education occurs at various times, not just in school.

    ___ **a.** Watching television can be very relaxing.

    ___ **b.** Newspapers and magazines can tell readers a great deal about current problems and events.

    ___ **c.** Education should be an on-going process, not something that takes place only in school.

    ___ **d.** Students should make the most of their years in school.

    ___ **e.** A job can provide an opportunity to learn about people.

2. Controlling Idea: Urban renewal causes displacement hardships for many people.

    ___ **a.** When an apartment house is torn down to make way for new buildings, people are often forced to relocate.

    ___ **b.** Sometimes, city government tries to find new housing for dislocated tenants.

    ___ **c.** In many ways, New York City is a difficult place in which to live.

    ___ **d.** Very often, when large buildings are put up, many small store owners are forced out of business or are forced to move.

    ___ **e.** In the past ten years, hundreds of new office and apartment buildings have appeared in most large cities.

3. Controlling Idea: A college education may provide a student with several advantages.

    ____ **a.** Many colleges have required courses that the students must take before they can begin to specialize.

    ____ **b.** Many older people are returning to school to continue their education.

    ____ **c.** College provides general information essential to many activities.

    ____ **d.** A college education is considered a necessity by many people today.

    ____ **e.** College can teach students special skills that will be useful in their chosen careers.

4. Controlling Idea: The current world population explosion is creating food and medical care shortages.

    ____ **a.** Many people believe in the policy of "zero population growth."

    ____ **b.** Many countries are finding it difficult to feed all their people.

    ____ **c.** In some countries, there are not enough doctors and nurses to care for all the people.

    ____ **d.** Many governments want people to know how to control the size of their families.

    ____ **e.** Overpopulation is just one of the many issues that governments are concerned about today.

5. Controlling Idea: I plan to get married for two reasons.

    ____ **a.** Marriage provides a chance to give and get affection.

    ____ **b.** Sometimes marriages do not work out, and divorce becomes the only solution to the problem.

    ____ **c.** Sometimes a person wants to live with another person but does not want to get married.

    ____ **d.** In earlier times, when marriages were arranged by parents, people seldom married for love.

    ____ **e.** Marriage offers an opportunity to share the pleasures and pains of life with someone else.

Activity 2 Writing Topic Sentences

Sometimes, inexperienced writers develop a topic sentence that says the same thing as the controlling idea but in different words. Such a topic sentence does not support the controlling idea; it merely restates it. The purpose of a topic sentence is to *back up* the controlling idea, not to repeat it.

Exercise 1   Read each controlling idea and then write two topic sentences, one for each of the two body paragraphs that would follow.

1. Controlling idea in introductory paragraph

   Drug addiction affects the mind and the body.

   WRITE topic sentence for first body paragraph

   _____

   _____

   WRITE topic sentence for second body paragraph

   _____

   _____

2. Controlling idea in introductory paragraph

   Violence on television can affect young children in several ways.

   WRITE topic sentence for first body paragraph

   _____

   _____

   WRITE topic sentence for second body paragraph

   _____

   _____

3. Controlling idea in introductory paragraph

   Fads in clothing can influence student behavior in school and at social functions.

   WRITE topic sentence for first body paragraph

   _____

   _____

WRITE topic sentence for
second body paragraph
   _____

_____

4. Controlling idea in
introductory paragraph
   Ex-alcoholics can help alcoholics in different ways.

WRITE topic sentence for
first body paragraph
   _____

_____

WRITE topic sentence for
second body paragraph
   _____

_____

5. Controlling idea in
introductory paragraph
   Cigarette advertisements
on billboards and in magazines often are misleading.

WRITE topic sentence for
first body paragraph
   _____

_____

WRITE topic sentence for
second body paragraph
   _____

_____

6. Controlling idea in
introductory paragraph
   Using fewer lights and less
heat in the winter helps to con-
serve energy.

WRITE topic sentence for
first body paragraph
   _____

_____

WRITE topic sentence for
second body paragraph
   _____

_____

7. Controlling idea in
introductory paragraph
   Participating in sports can
be beneficial to the physical
and mental health of a student.

WRITE topic sentence for
first body paragraph

_____

_____

WRITE topic sentence for
second body paragraph

_____

_____

8. Controlling idea in
introductory paragraph

Going to a local college
saves students money and
time.

WRITE topic sentence for
first body paragraph

_____

_____

WRITE topic sentence for
second body paragraph

_____

_____

SUMMARY

You will have little trouble with topic sentences if you remember that they are connected to the controlling idea. Topic sentences must follow logically from, and should strongly support, your controlling idea.

Lesson 5

Introductory Paragraphs

In This Lesson:

READ:

- to analyze the techniques used to begin an introductory paragraph.

WRITE:

- introductory paragraphs which employ the four common techniques used to begin such paragraphs.

In lessons 3 and 4 of this unit, we concentrated on controlling ideas and topic sentences. In Unit 1, we compared writing an essay to building a house. The controlling idea and topic sentence are similar to the foundation and frame of a house. You can also compare the process of writing an essay to the experience of meeting someone for the first time. In your opening remarks to a stranger, you will probably establish who you are and touch upon some subject which seems to interest you both. You may then discuss the subject for a short time. Finally, you will find some way of concluding your conversation. This is a *natural* process of beginning, developing, and ending a conversation. The same procedure should be used in writing an essay. In this section, you will now learn how to begin your "conversation" with your reader.

The introductory paragraph must do the following three things:

1. introduce the subject by arousing the reader's interest.
2. state the controlling idea.
3. state the plan of development; that is, tell how you will go about supporting your controlling idea.

Note: Some teachers do not require a plan of development. If your teacher does require a plan, it is usually the last sentence in the introductory paragraph. A typical plan would say "This essay will discuss two of the problems" or "We will now look at the reasons for the trend."

Activity 1 Arousing the Reader's Interest

Right now, we will concentrate on how to introduce the subject by arousing the reader's interest. You can do this in four ways.

1. Ask a question.
2. Tell why the subject is important.
3. Make a firm declaration.
4. Make a startling declaration.

Read the following samples and note the devices used to capture attention:

SAMPLE INTRODUCTIONS

DEVICES TO USE IN INTRODUCTORY PARAGRAPHS

Understanding Yourself

Are there things about yourself you do not understand? If so, you are not alone. Because human behavior is very complicated, many people fail to know themselves. There are several reasons for this.

INTRODUCTION: Ask a question and present your controlling idea.

The Importance of Friendship

Almost all people need help, which is to say, they need friends. When you need to relieve your mind and talk over personal problems, you need a person who understands you. Sympathetic friends can assist you in several ways.

INTRODUCTION: Tell why subject is important and present your controlling idea

Two of New York City's Most Serious Problems

The people of New York City have problems like those of others in many large cities. However, to know that other people suffer from hardships similar to those suffered in New York City is not much comfort. It is not going to make up for the fact that every day people who live in the "Big Apple" have to face the very serious problems of traffic congestion and air pollution.

INTRODUCTION: Make a firm declaration and present your controlling idea

A New Breakthrough for Women

Women have broken into another traditionally male-dominated area—the world of crime! Increasing numbers of women are carrying out, both alone and in groups, violent as well as nonviolent crimes.

INTRODUCTION: Make a startling declaration and present your controlling idea

Exercise 1

Read the following introductory paragraphs. Decide which introductory device is being utilized in each paragraph. Then write the name of that device in the blank space.

Paragraph A_____

Scientists have been studying the ways of using solar energy as an alternative energy source. They have long recognized that the energy sources we now depend on are not going to be available forever. Harnessing the energy of the sun, however, though a cause of optimism for the future, still presents many problems. In this essay, several of these problems will be discussed.

Paragraph B_____

Are you a "steak and potatoes" person? Do you believe that a beefsteak is a good way to get your daily protein requirements? Actually, the steak dinner that so many Americans love is neither the best source of protein nor the most efficient way of using the grain that we have in such abundance in this country. A steak dinner is too much of a good thing for the American diet and too little a good thing for the hungry people in other parts of the world. The reasons this is so will be explored here.

Paragraph C_____

Arson, the setting of fires, is growing to epidemic proportions. The number of arson fires now exceeds 100 000 a year, more than triple the rate of ten years ago. A crime that is difficult to prevent and easy to commit, it often results in a tragic loss of lives. Arson for profit has long been common, but most recently, the trend has been toward arson for revenge. This essay will look at two reasons for this trend.

—Adapted from *Newsweek*.

Paragraph D_____

American higher education attempts to provide students with a liberal education without requiring necessary discipline and hard work. This is wrong. There is joy in learning just as there is joy in sports, but both learning and sports require a lot of effort. Becoming an educated person is a difficult, demanding enterprise in many ways. This essay will explore two of these ways.

—Adapted from Steven M. Cahn, "The Myth of the Royal Road."

Exercise 2   For the paragraphs you have just read, write down the controlling ideas and plans of development:

Paragraph A: controlling idea: _____

plan of development: _____

Paragraph B: controlling idea: _____

plan of development: _____

Paragraph C: controlling idea: _____

plan of development: _____

Paragraph D: controlling idea: _____

plan of development: _____

Activity 2   Reading and Analyzing Various Introductory Paragraphs

In summary, a good introductory paragraph should do three things for the reader:

1. Introduce the subject by arousing the reader's interest.
2. State the controlling idea.
3. State the plan of development (although some teachers do not require that this be actually stated).

In a previous lesson, we used "cheating" as an example of a broad subject. Let's work up a controlling idea from this broad subject:

Broad Subject - - - - - - - - - - - - - Cheating
Slightly Limited Subject - - - - - Students Cheating at School
Limited Subject - - - - - - - - - - - Reasons for Rise in Students
                                                     Cheating at School
Controlling Idea—The reasons for the alarming rise in student
                          cheating are numerous.

Now let's use this basic controlling idea, with minor variations in wording, in four introductory paragraphs. Note that the plan of development (telling the reader exactly how your essay will proceed) is placed after the controlling idea. The particular method used in attracting the reader's interest is stated for each paragraph.

Paragraph A

ASKING A QUESTION

Have you ever been faced with a blank answer sheet and a blank mind? If you have, then you know the terrible feeling of panic and fear that can lead to cheating. You are not alone. Many students have this fear, and many cheat because of it. Actually, fear is only one reason for cheating. There are several other reasons for the alarming rise in cheating. This essay will explore two of them.

Paragraph B

MAKING A STARTLING STATEMENT

Everyone hates a cheater. Conscientious students, who study for tests, feel gypped when other students copy their answers and get the same grades. Teachers dislike cheating because it usually indicates that the students have not studied and do not know the work. Students who cheat always have to worry about being caught, and they often feel guilty about their cheating. Yet, student cheating is on the rise. The reasons for this rather alarming rise are numerous. We will explore several of these reasons in this essay.

Paragraph C

TELLING WHY THE SUBJECT IS IMPORTANT

Cheating is one of the most serious problems in our schools today. "Crib sheets" are common and so are notes written on hands, sleeves, and desks. School newspapers advertise places which will sell term papers. Some students who write their own papers are guilty of plagiarism, another form of cheating. Cheating is becoming more serious because it is so widespread, and the rate is rising. The reasons for this rise are numerous. This essay will investigate two of these reasons.

Paragraph D

MAKING A FIRM DECLARATION

Everyone of us, sometime or another, has had some experience in cheating. For most of us, the answer we obtained by cheating was not worth the guilty feelings, so we never cheated again. A growing number of students, however, has become dependent upon cheating and cannot make it through a test without getting answers from someone else's paper. The reasons for the alarming rise in student cheating are numerous. This essay will consider two of them.

Exercise 1   List the three items contained in an introductory paragraph:

1. _____

2. _____

3. _____

List the four methods used to attract the reader's attention:

1. _____

2. _____

3. _____

4. _____

Exercise 2   Read the three introductory paragraphs below and then answer the questions.

Paragraph A

Women are stronger than men! Impossible, you say. Everyone knows men have bigger muscles, can lift heavier objects, can run faster, and can jump higher than women. For the general population, this is true. But women are stronger in a different way. In physical health and endurance, women have been outdistancing men for years. Men have more heart attacks, suffer from more ulcers, and die sooner than women. Physiological differences and fewer cultural pressures are two reasons women live longer than men. First, let us consider the major physiological differences and then the cultural pressures.

1. How does this author attract your attention?

2. State the controlling idea found in this introduction.

3. What is the author's plan of development?

Paragraph B

Searching for happiness is one of the biggest problems facing people today. Everyone has unhappiness and pressure from which she or he wants to escape. Unfortunately, there is no one recipe for manufacturing happiness. This is something one must discover alone. Luckily, there are many different ways of achieving happiness. This essay will look at two of the ways.

1. How does this author attract your attention?

2. State the controlling idea found in this introduction.

3. What is the author's plan of development?

Paragraph C

Why do people dream? Do dreams serve any purpose besides entertaining us? Religious people say dreams are messages from God. Those who believe in Extrasensory Perception (ESP) think dreams may be warnings about future events. Scientists and psychologists have other theories on the reasons people dream. First, this essay will investigate the scientific theories and then those less scientific.

1. How does this author attract your attention?

2. State the controlling idea found in this introduction.

3. What is the author's plan of development?

Activity 3 Comparing the Introductory to the Developmental Paragraph

How is the beginning paragraph of an essay different from the body or developmental paragraphs? Read the following essay on alcoholism. After you have read it, go back to paragraph 1. Then look at paragraphs 2 and 3. Try to discover for yourself two or three ways in which paragraph 1 is different from the other paragraphs.

The Alcoholic Population

After a long, hard day, many people find comfort in an ice-cold beer or a martini. For some of these people, alcohol, in any form, is a dangerous drug. These people are alcoholics. Recently, doctors have been trying to discover what alcoholics are like and why people become alcoholics. This essay will report on what doctors have uncovered.

Doctors have discovered one misconception about what alcoholics are like. The popular picture of an alcoholic as a bum is wrong. Actual statistics show that these pathetic human beings make up only 3 percent of the alcoholic population. The majority of the 9 million American alcoholics are from middle-class homes and have good jobs. Alcoholics can be found on every level of society. Although most alcoholics are male, female alcoholism is a growing problem. Alcoholics come from all races, colors, and creeds.

One specific reason explaining why drinkers become alcoholics has not been found. If alcohol itself were the cause, everyone who drinks would become addicted. Some doctors believe emotional problems cause alcoholism; drinking is often used as a means of escaping from worries. Other doctors feel alcoholism stems from changes in body chemistry. This would mean a physical reason for alcoholism exists. In most cases, though, a combination of these reasons produces an alcoholic.

Much more remains to be learned about this serious problem. Continued cooperation between doctors and Alcoholics Anonymous can provide additional information about alcoholism. We all hope this illness will be controlled some day.

Your close reading and analysis should have revealed the following:

THE INTRODUCTORY PARAGRAPH:

1. INTRODUCES THE SUBJECT AND AROUSES INTEREST IN IT

   After a long, hard day, many people find comfort in an ice-cold beer or a martini.

2. PRESENTS A CONTROLLING IDEA (THESIS STATEMENT)

   Recently, doctors have been trying to discover *what alcoholics are like* and *why people become alcoholics.*

THE FIRST DEVELOPMENTAL PARAGRAPH:

1. CONCERNS ONE ASPECT OF A SUBJECT

   What alcoholics are like.

2. STATES THAT ASPECT IN ITS TOPIC SENTENCE

   Doctors have discovered one misconception about *what alcoholics are like.*

3. DEVELOPS THE TOPIC SENTENCE WITH REASONS AND DETAILS

> Pathetic human beings make up only 3 percent of the alcoholic population.
>
> The majority of the 9 million American alcoholics are from the middle-class homes and have good jobs.
>
> Alcoholics can be found on every level of society.

THE SECOND DEVELOPMENTAL PARAGRAPH:

1. CONCERNS ANOTHER ASPECT OF A SUBJECT
> *Why people become alcoholics.*

Now, you fill in the rest; follow the form set out above.

2. STATES THAT ASPECT IN ITS TOPIC SENTENCE

_____

3. DEVELOPS THE TOPIC SENTENCE WITH _____

_____

_____

_____

_____

_____

_____

Exercise 1—**Comparing Introductory and Developmental Paragraphs**
Here are three paragraphs taken from expository essays written on different subjects. Read through each paragraph carefully. Ask yourself whether it introduces the subject that will be discussed in greater detail in the following paragraphs, or whether it treats one aspect of a subject. If it is a more general introductory paragraph, write *I* in the box next to the paragraph number. If it is a more specific developmental paragraph, put a *D* in the box. The first one is done for you.

Paragraph A

☐ Rosalynn Carter proved to be ready for the press before her husband was inaugurated as President of the United States. When she was interviewed on the subject of her husband's character, she thought long and hard before she came up with her key to his personality. Finally she settled upon two aspects of his character that had made her husband who he is: his roots in Plains, and his constant hard work.

—Adapted from *Time*.

Paragraph B

☐ Another reason for the increase in premarital sex among teenagers is the ready availability of birth-control devices and pills. Years ago, teenagers were prohibited by law from purchasing birth-control devices. Today, these devices are openly displayed on drugstore counters and may be purchased by teenagers as well as by adults. Birth control pills, obtainable only through a doctor's prescription, are also available to teenagers. Clinics and many private doctors will prescribe "the pill" if they believe a young girl is in danger of becoming pregnant. Cases have even been reported in which mothers have put "the pill" in their daughters' orange juice as a safety precaution. With the rapid rise in teenage pregnancies and abortions, the American public seems to realize that "an ounce of prevention is worth a pound of cure."

Paragraph C

☐ Eating to live is better than living to eat. Americans, in general, eat too much and too foolishly. Chocolates, cheeseburgers, French fries, cokes, and pizza pies are the usual eating fare of many obese Americans. Doctors have found, however, that the Atkins and Stillman diets often help fat people to change their eating habits while they lose pounds rapidly.

Writing Introductory Paragraphs

As we said earlier, an introductory paragraph arouses interest in a general subject. This subject is then discussed in detail in the body or developmental paragraphs. Before you begin to write your own introductions, review the four ways of arousing interest in your subject.

Exercise 1   Select two controlling ideas that you wrote for previous lessons or write two new ones. For each controlling idea, write an introductory paragraph.

SUMMARY

The introductory paragraph has three tasks: it introduces the subject by arousing the reader's interest, it states the controlling idea, and it may state the plan of development.

Four ways to capture the reader's attention are as follows: (1) asking a question, (2) telling why the subject is important, (3) making a firm declaration, and (4) making a startling declaration. This introductory statement should lead into the controlling idea, which is sometimes followed by a statement setting forth the plan for developing the essay.

UNIT FOUR:

The Essay as a Whole

In this unit, you will be doing a lot of writing. All the knowledge and skills that you have acquired throughout this book will now be put to use.

Since you are soon to be writing your own four-paragraph essay, it makes sense to review the structure of an essay from Unit One. Then read the four-paragraph essay which follows and note the analysis on the right, which makes the basic structure clear.

Problems of Cities and Suburbs

The city and the suburbs once seemed to be very different places. A city meant tall buildings, honking taxis, and smog-filled skies. The suburbs, on the other hand, meant family homes, gardens and lawns, and clean air. The problems faced by cities and suburbs also seemed quite different. Nowadays, however, metropolitan and suburban areas share many of the same problems, such as crime and drug addiction.

Crime is one problem found in both urban and suburban areas. Elderly people are mugged whether they are hurrying along a city street or strolling down a suburban avenue. Residents living in cities and suburbs hide in fear behind double-locked doors, hoping to prevent rob-

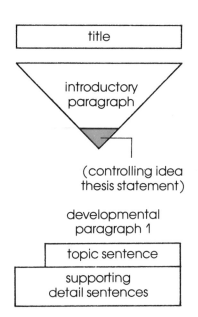

title

introductory
paragraph

(controlling idea
thesis statement)

developmental
paragraph 1

topic sentence

supporting
detail sentences

beries. In both the city and the suburbs, big, vicious dogs are used as additional protection against robberies. Even juvenile crime is a growing problem as gangs increase in the metropolitan and suburban areas.

Drug addition is another problem shared by cities and suburbs. Young people growing up in overcrowded, unpleasant city ghettos often turn to drugs, such as heroin, for a temporary escape from life. Suburban youngsters turn to drug addiction to search for kicks and to put excitement into their boring lives. Often they become addicted to another kind of drug, alcohol. Whether the drug is heroin, cocaine, or alcohol, it can be bought quite easily in either a city or a suburban school playground. Parents and officials in both areas are worried by the prevalence of drug addiction.

Our American cities and suburbs may still look different from each other. However, the problems facing these two areas today are really the same.

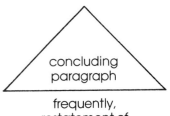

developmental paragraph 2

| topic sentence |
| supporting detail sentences |

concluding paragraph

frequently, restatement of controlling idea

Review   To be sure that you understand the structure of the essay, fill in the blanks with the correct word or words.

1. The controlling idea (thesis statement) tells the reader _____

_____

2. The sentence that tells the reader what each body or developmental paragraph is about is called a _____

3. The controlling idea in this essay is _____

_____

4. Topic sentence 1 is _____

_____

5. Topic sentence 2 is _____

_____

6. In the concluding paragraph, the restatement of the controlling idea is _____

_____

Lesson 1

Reading and Analyzing the Whole Essay

LOOKING AHEAD

In This Lesson:

READ:

- to analyze short essays for controlling ideas and for developmental and concluding paragraphs.
- to analyze body paragraphs organized in particular patterns.

WRITE:

- several four-paragraph essays.

Activity 1 Reading the Essay as a Whole

In the examples of four-paragraph essays that follow, you should read the essay through first to note the *main* (controlling) idea and the supporting topic sentences in the body paragraphs. Then, as you read it a second time, go over the analysis on the right-hand side. This running commentary will point out several organizational features you should note, such as controlling idea, plan of development, and topic sentences. In order to assist you further in noting the organization of the essay, a sample outline is presented to show you the "blueprint" of the essay.

Example 1

Planning and Organizing an Essay

What do blueprints and concrete have to do with writing an essay? Just as the first steps in building a house involve the drawing of blueprints and the laying of a foundation, so the first principles of good writing are forethought and organization. Without careful planning, an essay will wander; without a foundation of well-organized paragraphs, it will collapse. This essay will examine methods of planning and organizing a four-paragraph essay.

Introductory Device

Controlling Idea

Plan of Development

An essay should not be written until the author has thought about what he or she wants to say. Writing without thinking beforehand will result in windy prose that wastes words and fails to make its point clearly, if at all. Planning an essay consists of thinking about the steps necessary to make the point. All supportive material should be gathered during this stage, arguments should be formulated, and a sense of the conclusion should be established. Once these steps are accomplished, the writer is ready to organize the material.

Topic Sentence—". . . thought about what he or she wants to say."—"forethought" in controlling idea. Tells why forethought is important

Tells how an author should proceed *before* writing

Organization is the key to writing a good essay. Even if one has new and interesting information, a haphazard presentation will destroy its effect. Not only must a clear, concise controlling idea be followed by related topic sentences, but every sentence must follow every other, clearly and logically. No words should be wasted; everything

Topic Sentence—"organization" is repeated from controlling idea. Tells why organization is important.

Tells how an author should organize.

95

should pertain to the controlling idea of the essay.

If an essay is carefully thought out and organized, its creation is no more miraculous than the building of a house. Without careful forethought and organization, however, an essay is no more likely to stand than a house constructed without a proper foundation.

Restates the controlling idea by stating the idea in negative terms.

Now note how this essay was planned.

A SAMPLE COMPOSITION PLAN

Title: Planning and Organizing an Essay

Introduction

Introductory Paragraph

Arouse Interest in Subject: What do blueprints and concrete have to do with writing an essay?

State Controlling Idea: The first principles of good writing are forethought and organization.

State Plan of Development: This essay will examine methods of planning and organizing a four-paragraph essay.

Development

Body Paragraph 1

Topic Sentence: An essay should not be written until the author has thought about what he or she wants to say.

Body Paragraph 2

Topic Sentence: Organization is the key to writing a good essay.

Conclusion

Concluding Paragraph

Emphasize controlling idea to make clear its significance: Without careful forethought and organization, however, an essay is no more likely to stand than a house constructed without a proper foundation.

Exercise 1   Answer the following questions:

1. In your own words, state the main idea of the essay.

_____

_____

2. In your words, make clear how the author supports the main idea.

_____

_____

3. What conclusion does the author reach? _____

_____

_____

Example 2

William Shakespeare—Popular Then and Now

Ask anyone involved with English literature: "Who is the greatest writer?" and you will undoubtedly hear one name mentioned—William Shakespeare. Although Shakespeare died over 360 years ago, his thirty-seven plays are still valued and loved today. Why? Part of the answer lies in the fact that Shakespeare dealt with timeless problems that continue to concern us, such as prejudice and parent-child conflicts. This essay will discuss these problems, using several of Shakespeare's plays as examples.

The writer arouses interest by asking a question.

Notice that even a second question is used to maintain interest.

Controlling Idea

Plan of Development

Two of Shakespeare's best-known plays tackle the ugly and still unsolved problem of prejudice. The hero of *Othello* is a black soldier who marries a high-society white woman, Desdemona. Othello is clearly the best male character in the play. He is brave, successful, and talented; yet, most of the white people are horrified by his marriage. Because of unjustified prejudice, Desdemona's father also objects to their marriage. While straining against such prejudice, their marriage is preyed upon by Iago, one of Othello's officers, who excites Othello to become jealous of his wife. As a result, Othello and his wife tragically die. Shakespeare also worked with another form of prejudice, anti-Semitism, in *The Merchant of Venice*. The character Shylock is Jewish, and all the Christians curse him, hate him, and even spit on him. Even though Shylock is the villain, Shakespeare gives him many speeches to make it clear that Jews are also human beings.

Topic Sentence—*prejudice* is repeated from the controlling idea; *still unsolved* means that the matter still concerns us today.

Supporting-detail sentences provide examples of prejudice from *Othello* (prejudice against blacks) and *The Merchant of Venice* (prejudice against Jews).

Many of Shakespeare's plays are concerned with another still unsolved problem—the generation gap. For example, King Henry the Fourth, in the play of the same name, is a very cool, cynical, and snobbish politician. His son Prince Hal is just the opposite. Hal is warm and outgoing and is friendly with all kinds of people. He is also a "swinger" who goes to taverns and who plays around with women. Naturally, the father cannot understand the kind of life his son leads, and part of the action of

Topic Sentence—*generation gap* ties into the *parent-child conflicts* of the controlling idea.

Again, supporting-detail sentences back up the topic sentence by giving examples of parent-child problems in *King Henry the Fourth*, Part I (father-son problem) and *Cymbeline* (father-daughter problem).

98

the play *Henry IV* revolves around this parent-child difference. The play *Cymbeline* begins with another sort of parent-child problem. Here, the father, Cymbeline, wants his daughter Imogen to marry a man he likes. However, Imogen falls in love with someone else and secretly marries him. Cymbeline is furious. He orders the husband to go away, and he locks up his brokenhearted daughter. The rest of the play deals with the solution to this problem.

Shakespeare's plays are deservedly popular. They contain many colorful characters, beautiful poetry, and action-filled plots. Shakespeare's uncanny ability to focus on problems that are still current today also adds to the continuing success of his plays.

Restatement of controlling idea

A SAMPLE COMPOSITION PLAN

Title: William Shakespeare—Popular Then and Now

Introduction:

Introductory Paragraph

Arouse Interest in Subject: Ask anyone involved with English literature: "Who is the greatest writer?" and you will undoubtedly hear one name mentioned—William Shakespeare.

State Controlling Idea: Part of the answer lies in the fact that Shakespeare dealt with timeless problems that continue to concern us, such as prejudice and parent-child conflicts.

State Plan of Development: This essay will discuss these problems, using several of Shakespeare's plays as examples.

Development:

Body Paragraph 1

Topic Sentence: Two of Shakespeare's best-known plays tackle the ugly and still unsolved problem of prejudice.

Body Paragraph 2

Topic Sentence: Many of Shakespeare's plays are concerned with another still unsolved problem—the generation gap.

Conclusion:

> Concluding Paragraph

> Emphasize the controlling idea to make clear its significance: <u>Shakespeare's uncanny ability to focus on problems that are still current today also adds to the continuing success of his plays.</u>

Exercise 2   Answer the following questions:

1. In your own words, state the main idea of this essay.

_____

_____

2. Has the author helped you to better understand why Shakespeare remains popular today? _____

If so, how? _____

_____

3. Has the author convinced you to read some of Shakespeare's plays? _____

If so, how? _____

_____

If not, why not? _____

_____

Example 3

Why Study English?

Do you groan aloud when you think about studying English? If you answer "yes," you are not alone. Many students feel that studying English is a waste of time. They feel that once they get out into the real world, away from the classroom, English is not useful at all. This is definitely untrue. Now more than ever, a

Once again, a question is used to catch your interest. A question is a popular device because it is easy and dramatic.

Controlling Idea

good knowledge of English is important to help you get a job and to advance you in that job. First, we will consider how a good knowledge of English can help you to get a job. Then we will look at some ways in which your language skills can further your career advancement.

      Knowing English well can help you land the position you want. When you apply to a company, the first thing the potential employer sees is your résumé. If your résumé contains many spelling and grammatical errors, the company will probably toss it aside and take another résumé from the pile. Filling in an application form is the next step in getting a job. Once again, your ability to express yourself well, with no glaring errors in English, will be a plus on your side. The final step in getting a job is the personal interview. You have to make a good impression on your interviewer. If you mumble, if you can't talk in complete sentences, and if you can't develop your thoughts in a logical, coherent way, you probably won't get the job. In short, it pays to be attentive in your English classes.

      Once you do get a job, a good knowledge of English will help you to advance in your field. Your boss may give you written material to read, study, evaluate, and report on. You may also send in suggestions for improving company products or job conditions. If your reports and suggestions are well written, your employer will notice you and may even remember you at bonus

Plan of Development

Topic sentence—taken from the first part of the controlling idea

The supporting-detail sentences go in chronological order: résumé, application form, personal interview. These sentences back up the assertion made in the topic sentence.

Topic sentence—taken from the second part of the controlling idea

Supporting-detail sentences provide many examples of how English helps you after you get a job: your boss gives you material to comment on; you send in suggestions; you talk at a business meeting.

time. Whenever you appear at a business meeting, your supervisors will be watching what you say and how you say it. Any memorandums you send will also clearly demonstrate your ability to express yourself. A company on the lookout for people who qualify for advancement will be impressed if you can write and speak clearly and to the point. So, with all the competition in business today, you should know how to handle the English language well.

Studying English can bring you pleasure by giving you a sense of confidence. And don't forget that learning English well can help you first to get a job and then to advance in your career.

Restatement of the controlling idea

A SAMPLE COMPOSITION PLAN

Title: Why Study English?

Introduction:

Introductory Paragraph

Arouse Interest in Subject: Do you groan aloud when you think about studying English?

State Controlling Idea: Now more than ever, a good knowledge of English is important to help you get a job and to advance you in that job.

State Plan of Development: First, we will consider how a good knowledge of English can help you to get a job. Then we will look at some ways in which your language skills can further your career advancement.

Development:

Body Paragraph 1

Topic Sentence: Knowing English well can help you land the position you want.

Body Paragraph 2

Topic Sentence: Once you do get a job, a good knowledge of English will help you to advance in your field.

Conclusion:

Concluding Paragraph

Emphasize controlling idea to make clear its significance:
And don't forget that learning English well can help you first
to get a job and then to advance in your career.

Exercise 3   Answer the following questions:

1. In your own words, state the main idea of the essay.

_____

_____

2. Do you agree with the author's point about the importance of
English? If so, why? If not, why not? _____

_____

_____

_____

_____

_____

Exercise 4   Read the following essay and fill out a composition
plan for it.

Resolving Communications Problems

"I just can't talk to you" is a common complaint nowadays. Most
people have trouble communicating with others, and this causes grief and
unhappiness. A breakdown in communication is almost always caused
by people not listening carefully enough to one another and is solved by
their trying to understand what one another says. This essay will
discuss a reason and a remedy for communication problems.

The major barrier to effective communication is our tendency not to
listen to what another person has to say. We don't really pay attention
when we should, and we tend to "read into" statements meanings that
aren't there. For example, let's say that Mary saw movie A and adored it.
When someone close to her said that movie A was a bomb, she took that as
an insult to her taste and intelligence, and she got angry. She had no

reason to feel insulted simply because someone stated an opinion about movie A, but Mary didn't really listen to the actual statement. We all do similar things on occasion, and many relationships have crumbled because we haven't listened to each other.

Obviously, to break down communication barriers, we must listen to each other with care and understanding. To do this, we should listen *to* a statement, not listen *at* it. For example, Helen and Ed were on a date, and Ed was talking about some experience he had had in school several days before. If Helen had been listening, she might have gotten some insight into Ed or might have learned some interesting facts about him. Instead, she was thinking about an amusing anecdote that she could talk about when Ed finished speaking. By doing this, Helen really missed an opportunity to communicate with Ed. Also, many arguments are prolonged because of the communication barrier. In an argument, try to repeat what your opponent has said before you begin to react to it. You may discover that you didn't understand what was meant. If you succeed in presenting your opponent's argument accurately and fairly, then you have understood the other person's point of view. At that point, perhaps you can settle your differences with greater care.

These are examples of how we might remedy communication problems on a personal level. Can we take this knowledge and apply it to the larger failures of communication in the modern world? This is certainly a possibility and a challenge we should explore.

—Adapted from an essay by Carl R. Rogers.

Now fill in the blanks in the Composition Plan.

Title: _____

Introduction:

    Introductory Paragraph

      Arouse Interest in Subject: _____

_____

     State Controlling Idea: _____

_____

_____

    State Plan of Development: _____

_____

_____

Development:
Body Paragraph 1
  Topic Sentence: _____

  _____

Body Paragraph 2

  Topic Sentence: _____

  _____

Conclusion:
  Concluding Paragraph
  Emphasize controlling idea to make clear its significance:

  _____

  _____

Exercise 5   Read the following essay and fill out a composition plan for it.

Johnny's Parents Can't Read, Either

A woman in Colorado bought dog food for her family to eat. She wasn't buying dog food because she couldn't afford anything else. Instead, she bought the dog food thinking that it was meat because she wasn't able to read the label. This woman is one of the 23 million Americans aged sixteen and older who are functionally illiterate. These people can't read help-wanted ads, can't fill out forms for a driver's license or for Social Security, and can't read labels in a supermarket. But however terrible their problem is, it is curable. Most people can be taught to read if someone cares enough to teach them. Within the past ten years, people who do care enough about the illiterate have started several programs to help make readers out of nonreaders. This essay will discuss federal and nonfederal reading programs.

The federal program to help adult illiterates learn to read began in 1969, when the Office of Education launched the "Right to Read" program. Then, in 1975, funded by a federal grant of $1.4 million, eighty-two Reading Academies were set up all across the country. These academies stress individual, one-to-one tutoring by volunteers. The tutors include all types of concerned people: retired teachers, students, welfare clients, working people. Why do all these people volunteer? One Illinois tutor talks about the satisfaction found in helping others. He rejoices along with a student who, unable to read at all before starting the program, now reads, "dog . . . daddy . . . dig" for the first time.

In addition to this federal program, hundreds of concerned people have set up their own programs to help adult illiterates. One such man is Kenneth Craig, manager of a private business. He was shocked when he found out that 10 to 15 percent of his employees couldn't read. Mr. Craig was determined to help these people, so he hired a reading teacher and gave the workers time off to attend reading classes. He finds that learning to read gives his workers a sense of pride and dignity, which carries over to their jobs. Other nonprofit organizations work through libraries, churches, social-service groups—all sponsoring reading-instruction programs. Most of these programs are designed around specific needs. If someone wants to pass a driver's test, for example, then instruction is directed to that goal.

Because of decent, caring individuals in both federal and nonfederal programs, adult illiterates are getting a chance to change their lives. While it is a great achievement to teach someone how to read, some tutors hope for even more: to teach someone to love reading. A retired business executive, now a tutor in a nonfederal program, wants "to open the door for somebody to the wonderful world of literature."

—Adapted from an essay by Carl T. Rowan and David M. Magie, *Reader's Digest*.

Composition Plan

Title: _____

Introduction:
    Introductory Paragraph
        Arouse Interest in Subject:_____

_____

_____

        State Controlling Idea:_____

_____

_____

        State Plan of Development:_____

_____

_____

Development:
  Body Paragraph 1

    Topic Sentence: _____

    _____

  Body Paragraph 2

    Topic Sentence: _____

    _____

Conclusion:
  Concluding Paragraph
  Emphasize controlling idea to make clear its significance:

    _____

    _____

  Now answer the following questions about *Johnny's Parents Can't Read, Either:*

  1. How does the title fit the essay? _____

    _____

  2. What introductory device is used? _____

  3. From the controlling idea, copy out the subject, verb, and key term to be divided.

      a subject _____

      a verb _____

      a key term to be divided_____

  4. How are the topic sentences related to the controlling idea?

    _____

    _____

    _____

    _____

5. How do the supporting-detail sentences support the topic sentences?

_____

_____

_____

6. What device does the author use in the concluding paragraph?

_____

Activity 2 **Writing Your Own Essay**

You will now get a chance to display all that you have learned so far in this book. Before you begin to write your own essay, organize your thoughts in terms of an introductory paragraph, two body paragraphs, and a concluding paragraph.

Exercise 1   Write a four-paragraph expository essay reacting to one of the five essays you read above. Select *one* of the topics suggested below:

Essay 1—Perhaps writing reminds you of some activity other than building a house. Write an essay explaining your ideas.

Essay 2—Perhaps you thought of another author besides Shakespeare whose work will remain popular for many years. Write an essay using your author as an example.

Essay 3—Perhaps you don't agree with the essay "Why Study English?" If this is the case, write an essay explaining why one should not study English.

Essay 4—You may think that there are other barriers and also other gateways to communication besides the ones discussed. Write an essay giving your own ideas on the subject.

Essay 5—After reading "Johnny's Parents Can't Read, Either," you may have thought of some other way to combat the problem of adult illiteracy. Write an essay on your idea.

Exercise 2   Write a four-paragraph essay on any subject of your choice. Possible topics: one of your favorite authors, musicians, athletes, TV or movie stars. Remember to limit your subject before writing a controlling idea.

Activity 3   Analyzing Different Types of Essays

In Unit Two, we discussed three ways to organize paragraphs—by comparison-contrast, time order, and cause and effect. These three ways can also be the bases for organizing entire essays. In this section, you will read essays that use these three basic patterns. You will also read essays that will introduce two additional patterns—classification and definition.

Example 1:   Comparison-Contrast

If you are asked to compare two things, here is an example of the type of essay you might write.

Movies Then and Now

Movies are like a giant reflecting mirror. They reflect what we, the public, think and dream. As public attitudes change, so do the attitudes shown in the movies. For example, people today are cynical about war and heroism, so antiwar and antiheroic movies like *M*A*S*H* are more popular than the patriotic movies from earlier times. Movies of the 1930s differ drastically from movies of today in many other ways as well. This essay will contrast the use of off-color language and the treatment of sex in movies then and now.

In the 1930s, the attitude toward "questionable language" was simple—a movie rarely included such language. Let us use *Gone With the Wind*, an extremely popular movie of the '30s, as an example. In this film, Rhett Butler utters his closing lines—"Frankly, my dear, I don't give a damn"—to Scarlett O'Hara. This line is innocuous by today's standards, but it held up the production of the entire movie. Finally, special permission was given for the use of the word *damn*. In modern movies, on the other hand, four-letter words are commonplace. For example, *The Last Detail*, a Jack Nicholson movie, contains scarely one line of dialogue without off-color language. Movie audiences now accept this type of language; therefore, the movies make use of it.

Movies of the '30s also treated sex very differently from the way it is treated today. Then, only "bad" people had affairs while married, and sex before marriage was out of the question. A delightful comedy of that time, *It Happened One Night,* illustrates these views. A male reporter and a runaway heiress spend several nights together, forced to share a room. To make sure nothing happens, the reporter creates a barricade between the beds by hanging blankets over a clothesline stretched from wall to wall. Only during the last scene, when the two are legally married, does this "Wall of Jericho" come tumbling down. A comedy of the 1970s, such as Warren Beatty's *Shampoo,* provides the modern counterpart. In this movie, married couples have many affairs, and the single people go from one sex partner to another. Indeed, the whole treatment of sex is so "liberated" that mother and daughter even share the same lover. None of the characters in the movie seems shocked by these sexual adventures, and the silent audience simply accepts what is happening.

The United States has certainly changed a great deal since the 1930s. Our movies are evidence of this change. Modern movies, with their frank treatment of sex and their use of four-letter words, would shock an audience of the 1930s. In turn, some of the movies of that era seem refreshingly innocent to us today.

Example 2:   Process Analysis (similar to time order)

Frequently, it is necessary to explain to somebody how to do something. Here is an essay of the type you could write for that purpose. Its organization is known as *process analysis.* Note how the organization depends on the *time-order* pattern.

How to Read More Efficiently

Although most of us learned how to read years ago, the stark and awful truth is that most of us read laboriously and inefficiently. We crawl along at a rate of one hundred to two hundred words per minute and don't understand or remember much of what we've read. An efficient reader ought to fly along at six hundred to a thousand words per minute and ought to remember at least 80 percent of everything read! Reading specialists suggest several ways of increasing reading comprehension. This essay will consider two of these ways.

Always skimming written material first will ensure comprehension by helping you to see how the material is organized. With a textbook, try glancing at the table of contents first to get an overall picture of what the book will cover. Then, going chapter by chapter, read any lines in boldface print and read the summary that is often included at the end of the chapter. For a shorter piece of writing—an article or essay—try reading only the first sentence of each paragraph. Before long, you will be aware of the smooth and progressive flow of thought. When you have finished skimming in this way, you will be able to pinpoint the main ideas that the author is stressing. You will also have a rough idea of how the author is organizing the material to support the points being made. Skimming the material first will aid you in fully understanding the selection when you reread it later.

Another way to increase your reading comprehension is to give yourself tests. After you read something, see if you can tell yourself the details of what you have read. Can you enumerate the points in the order in which the author made them? Do you know the main idea of each paragraph? Could you coherently outline the author's thoughts without referring to the text? These kinds of questions will test your reading comprehension. Of course, you aren't expected to memorize and then recite all you read. But if you can't answer basic questions about the material, go back and read the selection again.

Reading is an extremely complex activity. The quickest way to improve your reading is to enlist the aid of a reading specialist. On your own, however, skimming a selection first and then testing yourself after reading can dramatically improve your reading comprehension.

—Adapted from an essay by Paul D. Leedy in the collection *The Wonderful World of Books*.

Example 3: Cause and Effect (causal analysis)

Causal analysis investigates the causes and effects of a specific thing (for example, the causes and effects of allowing eighteen-year-olds to vote). Here is an essay that discusses the cause and effect of TV game show popularity.

A Bit of Sadism after Lunch

Every afternoon, millions of people turn on their TV sets and settle down to watch the game shows. Besides these viewers at home, hundreds of other people are in the studio audiences, watching and cheering. The hundreds of applications that game shows receive from people hoping to be chosen as participants also point to the shows' popularity. But although game shows have become one of our national institutions, we should not be very proud of them. Examining one cause of the popularity of game shows and its effect will help to prove that these shows reveal the worst traits of people.

One cause of the popularity of game shows may be, at least in part, the humiliation that the viewers see and enjoy. There is no need to feel jealous of these contestants; they have no special ability, and they have

no dignity. Viewers, if they are human, have had their share of embarrass-
ment and have suffered blows to their self-esteem, and it doesn't hurt
a bit to see others getting theirs, especially on network television. An
audience that shrieks with delight when a contestant cries after trading an
$8000 car for an empty can is a sadistic audience. Game shows provide
an outlet for sadism, and that contributes to their popularity.

The effect of game shows is equally depressing. Viewers watch
unskilled contestants make a lot of money. These same viewers will begin
to think that wealth and success are due to dumb luck, not merit. Even
worse, contestants on "Let's Make a Deal," for example, who dress up like
chickens or clowns and jump up and down like trapped animals, are not
acting like human beings. They are degrading themselves and the people
who watch them. We try to teach our children that every human being
should be treated with dignity. But how can we view a hysterically
screaming contestant, willing to do anything for a chance to win some
silly prize, with dignity? The effect of game shows is destroying dignity,
the right of every human being.

It is true that sadistic traits are only one cause of game show popularity, and degradation of people only one effect. Still, these shows are a
national disgrace. In time, perhaps, the public will realize this, and then
the era of game shows will be over.

—Adapted from an article by Benjamin Stein in *The Wall Street Journal.*

Example 4: Classification

A helpful pattern for a writer to know is *classification*—taking a
large group (boys, girls, Democrats, people over thirty, people under
thirty) and breaking it up into smaller groups. The following essay
uses girls as the larger group and breaks this subject up into three
smaller groups.

The Secret System—How Boys Grade Girls

Girls have always wanted to know what boys talk about when they are
left alone. Well, at least part of the conversation centers around girls.
Girls are rated according to a system—a system that treats girls as status
symbols. This special classificatory system places girls in three categories. This essay will be a small investigation into these three types.

The first classification is the Knockout. This girl creates her best
effects at a distance. Her figure is stunning, and she dresses to emphasize it. The Knockout is an expert on timing. She enters a room at just the
right moment, almost like making an entrance on stage. She pauses at
just the right spot, framing herself in the scene. Most models and ac-
tresses are trained to do this. The Knockout knows how to do it naturally.
Elizabeth Taylor is probably the classic example of the Knockout.

The second classification is the Personality. She is vivacious—tossing her hair, laughing easily and charmingly, talking rapidly, always on the move. The effect she gives is winning and pleasant to everyone. The Personality has perfected the trick of getting a great deal of her personality into the atmosphere in a relatively short time. Unlike the Knockout, who stops the party by entering the room, the Personality tends to be a little "weird" deliberately. One good example is Shirley MacLaine.

The Dream is the last classification. This girl is likely to be quiet, even shy. Her voice is low, and she dresses conservatively. She isn't especially outstanding at a distance, and she may not project an electric personality, but she shines when you talk to her. The Dream doesn't like big parties. She would much rather be walking by the riverbed, watching the sunset, or reading a book of poetry in front of a winter fire. Audrey Hepburn could be classified as the Dream.

Even in the 1970s, in the midst of the Women's Liberation Movement, boys still put girls in these sexist-type categories. Perhaps if boys realize what they are doing, and if girls learn about what is going on, putting people in these types of categories will stop. In the near future, we hope that boys will look at girls and see different types of human beings—not Knockouts, Personalities, or Dreams. Of course, girls must be prepared to treat guys with the same respect.

—Adapted from an article in *Seventeen*.

Note: This essay has five paragraphs, not the usual four, but our original structure is retained (introductory paragraph, developmental paragraphs, concluding paragraph).

Example 5: Definition

At other times, you may write an essay defining something (usually something abstract) which means different things to different people, such as *love* or *happiness*. Here is one person's definition of *death*. Note, too, how the writer uses comparison and contrast to make the definition more vivid and meaningful.

Death—A New Definition

Every single one of us will die. It would seem, then, that we all should be eager to talk about death, but this isn't so. Instead, death is rarely discussed, perhaps because we hope if we ignore it, it will ignore us. Mostly, we are too afraid of death to talk about it. No one has ever returned from death to tell us what it is like. Recent medical advances, though, have made it possible for "dead" people to come back to life. The experiences of these people may change our thinking about death.

Indeed, our definition of death may have to be expanded. This essay will discuss the "old" and "new" definitions of death.

Death, in the usual definition, is the end of life. No thought, no feeling, no sense experience, no mental awareness is possible. The dictionary defines death as "a permanent cessation of all vital functions, a passing out of existence." Going along with this definition, most of us consider anything preferable to death. Even those who long for death—a terminally ill patient, for example—want to die only because it would mean the end of suffering. Poets often speak of death as an endless night. Death is like one long, dark night that will never brighten into day. No wonder many people fear death.

However, death, according to some recent research, may be the beginning of a new life, and not the end. While religious people have believed this for centuries, only now are researchers coming to this same conclusion. Dr. Raymond Moody, one such researcher, studied case histories of people who were pronounced "dead" but were later revived. The reports of these people mention certain experiences they had while "dead." They heard a strange noise, like a ringing, while they moved through a dark tunnel. They could look down at the hospital bed and see the doctors working on their bodies. Then, some sort of being, made up of light, came to them and filled them with peace and happiness. After that, they approached some sort of barrier. It is at this moment that the doctors revived their bodies. They usually did not want to return to life because, in contrast, death had been an experience full of joy and love.

A simple definition of death can't really exist. Depending on your experiences and your religious beliefs, death can either be something horrible or something wonderful, something to be afraid of or something to look forward to. We can never be absolutely sure which definition is correct, can we?

—Adapted from Raymond A. Moody, Jr., *Life After Life*.

SUMMARY

In this lesson, we have read essays and analyzed their structure. In this way, we saw how all the parts—introductory paragraph, controlling idea, topic sentences, developmental paragraphs, concluding paragraph—work together to form a well-organized, well-written expository essay. This lesson also gave examples of essays, each using one of five patterns: comparison-contrast, process analysis (time order), cause and effect (causal analysis), classification, and definition.

Lesson 2
The Concluding Paragraph

In This Lesson:

READ:

- the techniques used in concluding paragraphs.

WRITE:

- effective concluding paragraphs for expository essays.

Activity 1 **Reading and Analyzing Various Concluding Paragraphs**

A good essay should not end abruptly; it should have a conclusion that will give the reader a sense of finality of the thought's being completed. If the reader turns and looks for another page, something is wrong with the conclusion. The introduction is important because it gets the reader's interest. The conclusion is also important because it will stay in the reader's mind.

In most of the essays you have read so far, the concluding paragraph has restated the controlling idea. This is the most common use of the concluding paragraph. But there are three other ways to end the essay. The following are examples of all four devices that may be used in an essay's concluding paragraph.

| SAMPLE CONCLUSIONS | DEVICES TO USE IN CONCLUDING PARAGRAPHS |

Understanding Yourself   (Title)

Human beings are more complicated than the most sophisticated computers. For example, there are many influences on our behavior of which we are not aware. As you have read, one's behavior depends upon environment and past experiences.

Conclusion:
Restate controlling idea

The Importance of Friendship   (Title)

Sympathetic friends give you opportunities for relieving the stress and strain arising from problems. Sometimes they will give you new insights about possible solutions. At other times, by sharing your burden, they give you the assurance that someone cares. In short, friends offer you an opportunity to help yourself in a positive way.

Conclusion:
Tell the outcomes possible

Two of New York City's Most Serious Problems   (Title)

Does all of this mean that we should flee New York City? No! We should stay here. If we all left, there would be no one around to help the city survive.

Conclusion:
Ask a question

A New Breakthrough for Women   (Title)

Women have been treated as second-class citizens for a long time. We must change this and fight for the equality of all our people. Women must take their rightful places in all fields of society.

Conclusion:
Urge action or change

Earlier (page 85) we looked at four introductory paragraphs for an essay on cheating. Now let's keep the same subject and see four different concluding paragraphs, each using one device.

Paragraph A

Restate the Controlling Idea

It is not easy to eradicate student cheating because clear-cut reasons for the rise in cheating do not exist. Instead we face a complex situation in our classrooms. *The causes of the serious rise in student cheating are not simple or few.*

Paragraph B

State Possible Outcomes

This frightening rise in student cheating could have some dire results. If the cheating continues, all students will be suspected of being cheaters. Teachers will have students sit at alternate desks, while aides patrol the room, searching for cheaters. *In this prisonlike classroom, even the innocent will be considered guilty.*

Paragraph C

Ask a Question

We have just looked at several reasons for the alarming rise in student cheating. Perhaps now some progress will be made in dealing with this problem in our schools. *After all, students don't really want to cheat, do they?*

Paragraph D

Urge Action or Change

The recent upswing in cheating is alarming to educators, parents, and students. We have examined some of the reasons for this rise, but it is now time to do more than just examine the issue. *All concerned people must work together to stop this cheating.* "Noncheaters of the world—unite!"

Exercise 1   List the four devices that may be used in a concluding paragraph:

1. _____

2. _____

3. _____

4. _____

Exercise 2   As a review, list the four introductory devices that
may be used to attract a reader's attention. If you have trouble re-
membering them, see page 81.

1. _____

2. _____

3. _____

4. _____

Activity 2   Writing Concluding Paragraphs

In the following essay, read the introductory paragraph and the two developmental paragraphs. Then write four different concluding paragraphs.

Why Go to College?

Why go to college? There are many poor reasons for going to college.
Some students just drift into college for lack of anything better to do.
Other students feel that sitting in a classroom for four years is preferable
to facing the harsh realities of employment or unemployment. Still others
go to college for social reasons. However, I think the best reason for
attending college is the sincere desire to learn, that is, to obtain general
knowledge and specific skills.

College gives students general knowledge about many subjects.
Through required courses, students can broaden their understanding of
subjects that normally they might never study. Accounting students,

for example, may learn about areas as different from their own as art history and English literature. By the time students graduate, they will have had many chances to study ideas that shape the world and that contribute to what is known as "general culture." Well-educated and responsible adults, if they are to perform well in society, need diverse information about numerous subjects.

College also teaches students specific skills that will be useful in future careers. Courses such as computer science or business administration can train students in specialized skills that will help them find good jobs after graduation. Those who wish to enter such professions as medicine, law, engineering, or teaching receive their preliminary training in colleges. In addition, students in colleges can become budding experts in their major fields by taking elective courses. College, therefore, gives students many opportunities to prepare for a career.

Exercise 2   Here are the body paragraphs to a four-paragraph expository essay. Read them, and then write a variety of introductory and concluding paragraphs, following the directions given.

Title	**Let's Have Some Men's Liberation Also**
Body Paragraph 1	Men in America are not free to do some things that society expects of women. Although it is acceptable for a man to hammer and saw in public, few men have the nerve to knit or sew in front of others. Similarly, few men are free to admit that they might like to take care of children, cook, clean, and do other "househusband" chores. While women today are free to say that they prefer having paying jobs to being housewives, most men are not liberated enough to express their preferences.
Body Paragraph 2	Also, men in America are not free to express their emotions openly. For example, men are not supposed to cry even though they have the same tear ducts that women do. Few men allow themselves to cry at a friend's funeral or when watching a sad movie. Also, male friends who have not seen each other for a while cannot be openly affectionate when they meet again. They can only shake hands, or perhaps playfully punch each other, while jokingly calling each other names like "you old devil."

Write the following introductory paragraphs:

Title: Let's Have Some Men's Liberation Also

1. Write an introductory paragraph in which you *ask a question* and present your controlling idea.

_____

_____

_____

_____

_____

_____

2. Write an introductory paragraph in which you *tell why the subject is important* and present your controlling idea.

_____

_____

_____

_____

_____

_____

3. Write an introductory paragraph in which you *make a firm declaration* and present your controlling idea.

_____

_____

_____

_____

_____

_____

4. Write an introductory paragraph in which you *make a startling declaration* and present your controlling idea.

_____

_____

_____

_____

_____

_____

Now write the following concluding paragraphs.

Title: Let's Have Some Men's Liberation Also

1. Write a concluding paragraph in which you *restate your controlling idea.*

_____

_____

_____

_____

_____

_____

2. Write a concluding paragraph in which you *tell the possible outcomes* of what you have been discussing.

_____

_____

_____

_____

_____

_____

3. Write a concluding paragraph in which you *ask a question.*

_____

_____

_____

_____

_____

_____

_____

4. Write a concluding paragraph in which you *urge action or change.*

_____

_____

_____

_____

_____

_____

_____

Exercise 3   Take one of the controlling ideas you developed in the lesson on controlling ideas on page 61 or develop a new controlling idea. Write an essay from this controlling idea, paying attention to topic sentences, the introductory paragraph, and the concluding paragraph.

SUMMARY

We have learned that a good introductory paragraph should contain something to attract a reader's attention and should have a controlling idea and often a plan of development as well. The various ways to attract attention are : (1) to ask a question, (2) to make a startling declaration, (3) to make a firm declaration, or (4) to state the importance of the subject. Concluding paragraphs, which are important because they are your last chance to "grab" your reader, should have a sense of finality. Some effective devices you can use in your closings are: (1) to restate your controlling idea, (2) to ask a question, (3) to state the possible outcomes, or (4) to urge action or change.

Lesson 3

Revisions and Final Copy

LOOKING AHEAD

In This Lesson:

READ:

- a sample composition in its original and revised form.
- the checklist thoroughly.

WRITE:

- your composition and revise it.

Activity 1　Reading an Original and a Revised Essay

Right now, you may be asking: "Why do I have to revise my paper? I thought about my subject; I planned my essay and I wrote it. Why do I have to do anything else?" There are many reasons why it is a good idea to revise your original draft. The simplest reason is that human beings are imperfect. Everybody makes grammatical or spelling mistakes from time to time. Doing a revision helps you catch these mistakes before you hand in your paper. Errors caught on a second look can range from a simple punctuation error to a major problem such as an unclear controlling idea.

Another reason for revision is that you can see things more clearly if you read your paper another time. When you are writing, you may know what you mean, but a reader may not understand what you are trying to say. A revision can help make your thoughts clearer to your readers. You may also remember to add another example or some details that you had forgotten in the first draft. Or you may find that you have simply changed your mind about something.

Remember, the members of a rock group don't cut a record on their first try. They practice and do "take after take" until they are satisfied. Then they record. Why should you hand in a first draft when you can hand in a revised copy of your own "hit" record?

In the example below, you will read an original draft of a student's essay. As you read it, notice the errors and think about how you would revise this essay.

Sample Composition by a Student—Original Draft

Why Get Married?

Line Number
1   Some poeple maintain that the institution has
2   already gone out of style and is now facing extinction.
3   Although two people living together may not need a
4   marriage license, a couple planning to have children
5   should obtain one.
6   A child who bears the family name will feel
7   more emotionally secure than one who doesn't. When
8   a woman is admitted to a hospital before giving birth,
9   one of the first questions asked of her is whether of not she is
10   legally married, from this moment on, if the mother is unmarried the
11   illegimate child is forced to bear the unpleasant, and
12   sometimes painful, burden of being a "bastard."
13   A lack of parental can lead to a sense of loss and rejection
14   that will always trouble the illegitimate child
15   and further isolate her or him from the rest
16   of society.
17   Financial security is likelier for a child
18   of a legal marriage. While the parents are together, the
19   child will probably be taken care of. Even if the
20   parents are not married. Couples just living together
21   often remain together as long as married couples, even if
22   they don't have a license. But if a married couple separate,
23   then the father is still required to provide some means of child
24   support. He cannot simply decide to cut himself off from
25   the problems of raising the child, for he is forced by
26   law to continue to fulfill his responsabilities. In the
27   event of the father's death, the legitimate child is a
28   rightful heir to the estate and can inherit whatever
29   is his or her due share.
30   Although marriage may be advisable for a man and woman
31   living together, it is important for a couple planning
32   to become parents.

Exercise 1   Now the student reread the draft of the essay and noticed some things that should be changed.   Here is the list.   Place a *D* on the blank of each error in organization and development.   Place an *M* on the blank of each error in spelling, punctuation, or mechanics.

a. ___ The first paragraph doesn't capture the reader's attention.

b. ___ On line Number 1, *poeple* should be *people*.

c. ___ On line Number 1, it is unclear to which institution the writer refers.

d. ___ The controlling idea is not clear and needs to be redone.

e. ___ On line Number 9, the second *of* should be *or*.

f. ___ On line Number 10, "From this moment on" should begin a new sentence, thereby correcting the sentence run-on.

g. ___ On line Number 13, the sentence beginning "A lack of parental . . ." doesn't really follow the sentence before it.   A sentence or two should be added.

h. ___ On line Number 13, a noun is missing after *parental*.

i. ___ On line Number 17, some transition word, perhaps a word of addition, could be used to begin the second developmental paragraph.

j. ___ On line Number 19, the sentence beginning "Even if . . ." is a fragment.   This must be changed.

k. ___ On line Number 20, the sentence beginning "Couples just living together . . ." does not follow the idea of the paragraph.   It should be taken out.

l. ___ On line Number 26, *responsabilities* is spelled wrong.

m. ___ On line Number 26, the sentence beginning "In the event . . ." could use a transition word to make the sentence more coherent.

n. ___ On line Number 30, again, a transition word or phrase at the opening of the last paragraph might help.

o. ___ The whole concluding paragraph needs more force.

Now let's see the revised essay.   The letters you will notice refer to the errors above, which are also lettered.   For example, in the original on line Number 1, error "b" was a spelling mistake—*people*.   Now, in the revised essay, *people* has a "b" above it to show how the mistake was corrected.

Why Get Married?

Is a marriage license still important?[a]   Some _people_[b] maintain that
the institution of _marriage_[c] has already gone out of style and is now facing
extinction.   Although two people living together may not need a marriage
license, a couple planning to have children should obtain one _in order to_[d]
provide their offspring with emotional and financial security.

A child who bears the family name will feel more emotionally
secure than one who doesn't.   When a woman is admitted to a hospital
before giving birth, one of the first questions asked of her is whether _or not_[e]
she is legally married.   _From_[f] this moment on, if the mother is unmarried
the illegitimate child is forced to bear the unpleasant, and sometimes
painful, burden of being a "bastard."   _Only a rare father will give this_[g]
child the same amount of love and warmth that he would give to a child
of a legal marriage.   Some mothers also may not make a full commitment
of love to an illegitimate child.   A lack of parental _attention_[h] can lead to
a sense of loss and rejection that will always trouble the illegitimate child
and further isolate her or him from the rest of society.

Financial security is _also_[i] likelier for a child of a legal marriage.
While the parents are together, the child will probably be taken care _of,_[j]
even[k] if the parents are not married.   But if a married couple separate, then
the father is still required to provide some means of child support.   He
cannot simply decide to cut himself off from the problems of raising the
child, for he is forced by law to continue to fulfill his _responsibilities._[l]

m
Furthermore, in the event of the father's death, the legitimate child is a

rightful heir to the estate and can inherit whatever is his or her due share.
                    n
To sum up, although marriage may only be advisable for a man

and woman living together, it is important for a couple planning to become
                              o
parents. *The two adults involved must consider not only what is best for*

them but also what will be best for their child.

Activity 2   The Checklist

Here is a list of specific points to consider in revising your essay. As you revise your paper, check off each point when you can give a "yes" answer to the question.

1. Does my introduction capture the reader's interest?
2. Have I stated my controlling idea clearly?
3. Do my developmental paragraphs support my controlling idea?
4. Do my developmental paragraphs have unity and coherence?
5. Do my developmental paragraphs include specific nouns, forceful adjectives, and statistics where appropriate?
6. Does my concluding paragraph have force and finality?
7. Is my grammar correct?
8. Have I checked my punctuation, mechanics, and spelling?

Exercise 1   Look over the revisions of the essay "Why Get Married?" Discuss how those revisions fit the checklist.

It is always easier to see the mistakes on someone else's paper. However, you are now going to work with your own writing. Try to be objective; that is, pretend you are reading someone else's paper *or* pretend you are an editor or teacher reading a paper. Don't be afraid to cross out sentences or words that don't belong.

Activity 3   The Guidelines

In addition to checking the *content* and *style* of the paper, you need to check the *format*.   Here are some guidelines:

1. Always write on one side of the paper.
2. If you are typing your essay, double space to leave room for the teacher's comments.
3. If you are not typing, remember to write legibly and neatly. Also, remember to skip every other line to leave space for the teacher's comments.
4. Leave a 1½-inch margin on the left side of the paper and a 1-inch margin on the right.
5. Put the title of your essay on the top of the first page.
6. Number all your pages.
7. Do a final proofreading before handing in your essay.
8. Make sure your name is on every page.

Exercise 1   Select one of your own four-paragraph essays.   Reread it and revise it: think about your controlling idea, your topic sentences, how one sentence follows another, your grammar, and so on.

Use the checklist on page 128 and the above guidelines in Activity 3. In the checklist, answer each question, referring to the composition you are revising. You should be able to answer "yes" to each question. If some of your answers are "no," go back and work on your essay.

SUMMARY

Revision can be as important as the actual writing of your essay. A second (or even third) look at your work helps you to notice mistakes. Even if the mistakes are as minor as transposed letters (*poeple* for *people*), you must correct these mistakes before handing in your essay. By using the checklist for content and style and the guidelines for format, you can help to make your essay as good as it can be.

SECTION 2
GUIDE
TO
REVISING PAPERS

To the student:

    This Guide has been designed to help you understand the correction symbols placed in the margins of your compositions by your instructor. The symbol with its meaning appears on the left side of the Guide, and a fuller explanation, indicating how the symbol should be used in correcting papers, appears on the right. In many instances, examples of incorrect and correct usage are provided for your better understanding of these correction symbols.

Table of Contents to Guide

Ab *(abbreviation)*   **Write in full the abbreviation marked.**

Incorrect: *N.Y.* is the largest *&* most populated city in the *U.S.*

Correct: New York is the largest and most populated city in the United States.

Note: Some abbreviations are acceptable in formal writing. When used with proper names, titles such as Dr., Mr., Ms., Jr., Sr., and St. are correct. Other acceptable abbreviations are A.M., P.M., A.D., and B.C. The initials of certain organizations (AFL-CIO, AAA, NFL) and federal agencies (FBI, CIA, FDA) are also acceptable.

Cap *(capitalization)*   **Capitalize the word marked.**

Some Rules of Capitalization

RULE	EXAMPLE
Capitalize the first word of every sentence.	The house is haunted.
Capitalize proper names of persons.	Susan B. Anthony fought to win the vote for women.
Capitalize proper names of places.	New York and New Jersey are two of our largest industrial states.
Capitalize languages, religions, the names of historical events and institutions.	Many Californians speak English and Spanish.
	World War II ended in 1945.
	Episcopalians and Roman Catholics have many of the same ceremonies.
	Columbia University is larger than Hunter College.

Ca (case)   **Rewrite the sentence using the correct pronoun case.**

PRONOUN CASE

	SUBJECTIVE		OBJECTIVE		REFLEXIVE		POSSESSIVE	
	Sing.	Plural	Sing.	Plural	Sing.	Plural	Sing.	Plural
First Person	I	we	me	us	myself	ourselves	my mine	our ours
Second Person	you	you	you	you	yourself	yourselves	your yours	your yours
Third Person	he she it	they	him her it	them	himself herself	themselves	his her hers its	their theirs

Subjective Case:

Incorrect: Pat and *me* are going to school.
               Us students are going to school.

               (The pronouns in these sentences function as subjects. When in doubt, test for correct pronoun case by using the pronoun alone. "Me is going to school" and "Us are going to school" are obviously incorrect.)

Correct: Pat and I are going to school.
               We students are going to school.

Incorrect: I am smarter than *him*.
               I write as well as *her*.

               (A pronoun used in the second part of a comparison is the subject of an understood verb and must be in the subjective case.)

Correct: I am smarter than he [is].
               I write as well as she [does].

Objective Case:

Incorrect: The letter was for *he.*
               The candy was divided among *we* children.

               (The objective case is always used after a preposition. *For* and *among* are prepositions, and the pronouns following should be in the objective case.)

Correct: The letter was for him.
               The candy was divided among us children.

Reflexive Case:

Incorrect: I had only *me* to blame.
               He talks to *hisself* all the time.
               The girls know how to take care of *theirselves.*

               (The reflexive pronoun is used when the doer and the recipient of the action are the same person. Note: *hisself, theirselves,* and *themself* are not correct. The correct pronoun forms are *himself* and *themselves.*)

Correct: I had only myself to blame.
               He talks to himself all the time.
               The girls know how to take care of themselves.

Possessive Case:

Incorrect: That book is very old. *It's* pages are turning yellow.
               Mary said the car was *her's.*
               Is the book *your's?*

               (The possessive form of personal pronouns never takes an apostrophe. Note: *it's* is a contraction for *it is* or *it has.*)

Correct: That book is very old. Its pages are turning yellow.
               Mary said the car was hers.
               Is the book yours?

DM *(dangling modifier)*

The section marked is a dangling modifier. Rewrite the sentence in either of the following ways: (1) change the sentence so that the doer of the action immediately follows the modifier; or (2) revise the sentence completely by changing the dangling modifier into a subordinate clause.

Incorrect: *To find the correct meaning of a word,* a dictionary should be used.

(*You* is the doer of the action and must be included in the main clause of the sentence.)

Correct: To find the correct meaning of a word, you should use a dictionary.

Incorrect: *Running across the street,* the taxicab hit the boy.
(Was the taxicab running across the street?)

Correct: As the boy was running across the street, a taxicab hit him.
(The dangling modifier has been changed into a subordinate clause.)

Frag *(fragment)*

Rewrite the marked fragment by joining it to another sentence or by making it into a complete sentence.

Incorrect: People would smoke pot in public. *If marijuana is legalized.*

("If marijuana is legalized" is a subordinate clause and should be linked to the previous sentence. A subordinate clause is usually most effective when placed at the beginning of the sentence.)

Correct: If marijuana is legalized, people would smoke pot in public.

Incorrect: They love rich foods. *Such as vegetables cooked in cream sauces.*

(The fragment marked is an explanatory phrase and should be joined to the previous sentence.)

Correct: They love rich foods, such as vegetables cooked in cream sauces.

Incorrect: Having children is one of the rewards of marriage. *Seeing children come into the world. Watching them grow year by year. Helping them to reach independence.*

    (All the elements marked are fragments. *Seeing, watching,* and *helping* are participles, not verbs. The passage should be rewritten.)

Correct: Having children, watching them grow year by year, and helping them to reach independence are some of the rewards of marriage.

Incorrect: *The man who talked for an hour not realizing everyone was bored.*

    (This fragment has no verb. It can be corrected by eliminating the relative pronoun *who* or by changing the participle *realizing* into a verb.)

Correct: The man talked for an hour, not realizing everyone was bored. (OR) The man who talked for an hour did not realize everyone was bored.

K (*awkward*)   Rewrite the marked word, phrase, or passage to make the wording more effective.

An individual who smokes should realize that smoking two packages of cigarettes a day is reducing eight years of expectancy off his or her life.

(This sentence is awkward. Not only is it wordy, but it falsely implies that all smokers smoke two packages of cigarettes a day. It should be rewritten.)

Improved: The life expectancy of a heavy smoker is eight years shorter than that of a nonsmoker.

---

lc (*lower case*)   The marked word should not be capitalized.

(See section on capitalization for Rules of Capitalization.)

Mng (meaning) The marked word has been misused. Consult a standard-sized dictionary to find a word more exact, more appropriate, or more effective.

Incorrect: Scientists predict that cockroaches will *overtake* the world.

(*Overtake* means to catch up with; *overrun* means to infest or to swarm over.)

Correct: Scientists predict that cockroaches will overrun the world.

Incorrect: Sometimes when a married woman wants to work outside the home, her *old man* objects.

(*Old man* meaning "husband" is a slang expression and is not appropriate in formal writing.)

Correct: Sometimes when a married woman wants to work outside the home, her husband objects.

Incorrect: The *acquisition* of women into the job market has been beneficial to the economy.

(*Acquisition* is an inappropriate choice of word. *Entry* would be better.)

Correct: The entry of women into the job market has been beneficial to our economy.

Incorrect: A great *amount* of students attended the financial aid meeting.

(*Amount* is used when the quantity is not countable. Ex: a small amount of sugar. Use *number* when things or people can be counted.)

Correct: A great number of students attended the financial aid meeting.

Org (organization) Rewrite the marked passage by organizing the elements into a unified and coherent pattern.

Org

Loneliness is a special problem for the aged in New York City. There are many people who are suffering from this condition. Old age is a result of loneliness. The aged are segregated and discriminated against. In many ways, they are misunderstood. Many are placed in institutions and forgotten about. Others are left alone because of the mobility of their families. Bad health is another problem for our aged. Many are not able to function as they once did. Thus, they are lonely. They are also easy prey for criminals. This is a problem that most of our aged have to worry about. Loneliness is a serious problem for the aged in such a large city.

Comment

The first sentence, or topic sentence, should state the main idea of a paragraph, and the supporting sentences should develop this idea. In the above paragraph, the topic sentence tells the reader that the paragraph will discuss loneliness as a special problem of elderly New Yorkers. However, the supporting sentences do not develop this idea. Although the paragraph discusses the loneliness of the elderly, it does not relate this loneliness to the problems of living in a large city like New York. Also, the phrasing in the paragraph is often repetitive, and necessary connections between ideas are not made. Material unrelated to the topic sentence is also introduced. Although it is true that elderly New Yorkers are easy prey for criminals, the writer does not show how this relates to the topic of loneliness. Furthermore, the statement that "old age is a result of loneliness" is simply not true. The paragraph must be rewritten in its entirety.

Reorganized and Improved

Loneliness is a particular problem for elderly New Yorkers. City apartments are often small and expensive, and many New Yorkers place the older members of their families in institutions to make room for the younger generation. Many of these same families eventually escape from the crowded city to the suburbs and leave their elders behind. Shut away in institutions and deserted by their families, these elderly New Yorkers experience feelings of acute loneliness. Older citizens in the city who can still afford their own apartments are not much better off than those in institutions. New York is a city of high-rise apartment complexes and walk-up tenement dwellings. The aged, who are often infirm, find it difficult to cope with long corridors and steep stairwells. Thus, they too are shut in, isolated from family and friends. Loneliness and aging are problems most of us face sooner or later. And in New York City, these problems usually go hand in hand.

P (*punctuation*)   **Add the correct punctuation where indicated.**

Check your use of periods, commas, and other punctuation marks. Have you neglected to use punctuation, or have you used it incorrectly?

[*'*] (*apostrophe*)   **Insert an apostrophe where marked or remove an unnecessary apostrophe.**

Some Rules for Using the Apostrophe

1. Apostrophes are used to indicate possession:

Add the apostrophe and *s* to singular words to indicate possession.	Rita's sweater is on the chair.
Add the apostrophe and *s* to plural words which do not end in *s*.	The children's books are on their desks.
Add only the apostrophe to plural words ending in *s*.	You will need your parents' permission if you want to go to the dance.

2. Apostrophes are used in contractions to show that one or more letters have been omitted.

I don't know why my parents won't let me go on the picnic.

(I do not know why my parents will not let me go on the picnic.)

Some common contractions are: *can't, don't, haven't, I'll, I'm, isn't, it's, shouldn't, won't,* and *we're*

Note: *It's* is a contraction for *it is* or *it has.* *Its* is a possessive pronoun.

Example: It's a nice day today. (*It's* is a contraction for *it is.*)
The book is old. Its pages are yellow. (*Its* is a possessive pronoun.)

[,] (comma)   **Add a comma at the place marked.**

Some Rules for Using Commas

1. Commas are used before the conjunctions *and, or, nor, but, yet,* and *for* when they join coordinate clauses.

We will fight for our rights as students, and I predict we will win.

2. Use a comma after long introductory clauses and phrases.

Clause: *After we had eaten some raw clams at Coney Island,* we were sick.

Phrase: *To find the correct meaning of a word,* you should consult a dictionary.

3. Use a comma to separate items in a noun series or to separate a series of adjectives modifying the same noun. (The comma before *and* is optional.)

Noun series: *John, Mary, and Salena* are old friends.

Adjective series: The *short, smiling, bald* man in the corner is my teacher.

4. Use a comma to set off appositives and nonrestrictive clauses.

An appositive is a noun or its equivalent that adds to the meaning of a previous expression.

Jimmy Carter, *the President of the United States,* was born in Georgia.

A nonrestrictive clause is one which if omitted would not drastically change the meaning of the sentence.

Lunch, *which is usually served at noon,* will be served at 1:00 P.M.

[no ,] (no comma)   **Remove an unnecessary comma.**

1. A comma is not used between two items in the same clause joined by *and* or by *or.*

Michael's mother and Sue's father are old high school sweethearts.

She is either the secretary or the treasurer of the club.

2. Do not use commas to separate restrictive clauses from the rest of the sentence. (A restrictive clause is one which is necessary to the meaning of the sentence.)

Students who do not study will probably fail. (The restrictive clause "who do not study" identifies those students who will probably fail.)

[;] (*semicolon*) Add a semicolon where indicated to separate coordinate clauses.

1. A semicolon is used to separate coordinate clauses that are not joined by a conjunction.

New friendships are often made over a cup of coffee; old friendships are often renewed.

2. A semicolon or a period is necessary before words such as *however, therefore, consequently,* and *nevertheless* when they occur between independent clauses.

The students could not start the car; therefore, they walked home. (OR) The students could not start the car. Therefore, they walked home.

Pl (*plural*) Change the noun marked to the plural form.

Incorrect: Children should be encouraged to pursue their *ambition.*

(As there is more than one child, there is more than one ambition.)

Correct: Children should be encouraged to pursue their ambitions

---

Pro Agr (*pronoun agreement*) Identify the word (antecedent) to which your pronoun refers and make sure the pronoun agrees in number with this word.

Incorrect: Each of the candidates promises to keep *their* campaign pledges.

(Words such as *each, everyone, everybody, anyone, anybody, nobody, no one, either,* and *neither* are considered to be singular in number, so the pronouns that refer to them should also be singular.)

Correct:	Each of the candidates promises to keep his (or her) campaign pledges. (OR) All the candiates promise to keep their campaign pledges.

Ref *(reference)*   **Change the marked pronoun so that it clearly refers to a previous noun. Where necessary, substitute a noun for the pronoun or rewrite the sentence.**

Incorrect:	Rachel visited her aunt when *she* was in Chicago.
	(Who was in Chicago, Rachel or the aunt?)
Correct:	When Rachel was in Chicago, she visited her aunt.
Incorrect:	Gerald didn't know how to get to the Municipal Zoo until I wrote *it* down.
	(If the antecedent cannot be substituted for the pronoun, the sentence should be revised. In the above sentence, *it* refers to directions and not to *Municipal Zoo.*)
Correct:	Gerald didn't know how to get to the Municipal Zoo until I wrote the directions down.
Incorrect:	We were having a great time at the picnic when it started to rain. It depressed our spirits for a while, but we finally decided to go on with *it* despite the weather.
	(In the above passage, *it* is first used as an expletive and is then used to refer to both *rain* and *picnic*. The passage should be rewritten to avoid the confusion in pronoun reference.)
Correct:	We were having a great time at the picnic when it started to rain. The rain depressed our spirits for a while, but we finally decided to go on with the picnic despite the weather.

RTS *(run-together sentence)*   **Two independent clauses have been run together without proper punctuation.**

Run-together sentences may be corrected as follows:

1. by using a period after the first independent clause;

Incor:	The students are in the class-room they are taking a test.
Cor:	The students are in the class-room. They are taking a test.

2. by adding a semicolon after the first independent clause;

| Incor: | The couple lost their traveler's checks, therefore, they can't go to Florida. |
| Cor: | The couple lost their traveler's checks; therefore, they can't go to Florida. |

3. by using a comma with a coordinating conjunction (*and, but, yet, for, nor, or, so*);

| Incor: | The students want to have a party, they will need the teacher's permission. |
| Cor: | The students want to have a party, but they will need the teacher's permission. |

4. by making one of the clauses dependent.

| Cor: | If the students want to have a party, they will need the teacher's permission. |

Sp (spelling)

The marked word is misspelled. Consult a dictionary for the correct spelling.

Keep a list of the words you have misspelled to avoid making the same mistake again. For help in spelling, see page 215.

S-V Agr (subject-verb agreement)

Identify the subject and make the verb agree in number.

Incorrect: She *do* like to dance.

(The third person singular present tense (*he, she, it*) always takes a singular verb; and the singular verb, whether regular or irregular, always ends in *s*.)

Correct: She does like to dance.

Incorrect: The days of easy living *is* gone.

(In this sentence, *days* is the subject and requires the plural verb *are*.)

Correct: The days of easy living are gone.

Incorrect:	Pedro and Rosetta *is* getting married in June.
	(In this sentence, there are two subjects: Pedro and Rosetta. Therefore, the sentence requires the plural verb *are*.)
Correct:	Pedro and Rosetta are getting married in June.
Incorrect:	The questions of the child, which *is* often confusing, are always answered by her parents.
	(In this sentence, *which* refers to the subject *questions* and takes a plural verb.)
Correct:	The questions of the child, which are often confusing, are always answered by her parents.
Incorrect:	After marriage *comes* the fights.
	(In this sentence, the subject *fights* follows the verb. *Fights* is plural and requires a plural verb.)
Correct:	After marriage come the fights.
Incorrect:	There *is* five boroughs in the city of New York.
	(In this sentence, *there* is not the real subject. In a sentence beginning with *there*, the number of the verb always agrees with the subject that immediately follows the verb. *Boroughs* is a plural subject and takes a plural verb.)
Correct:	There are five boroughs in the city of New York.
Incorrect:	Either Jennifer or the twins *wants* more cake. Neither the twins nor Jennifer *want* more cake.
	(In sentences that use the constructions *either-or* and *neither-nor*, the verb agrees in number with the subject immediately preceding it.)
Correct:	Either Jennifer or the twins want more cake. (The plural subject *twins* immediately precedes the verb. Thus the verb is plural.)
	Neither the twins nor Jennifer wants more cake. (The singular subject *Jennifer* precedes the verb. Thus the verb is singular.)

T (tense)   **The tense of the marked verb is not consistent with other verbs in the passage, or an incorrect form of the tense has been used.**

Incorrect: For many years, I have been eating my mother's cooking and *loved* every bite of it.

(The past tense *loved* is not consistent with the present progressive tense *have been eating.*   Both verbs should be in the same tense.)

Correct: For many years, I have been eating my mother's cooking and loving every bite of it.

Trans (transition)   **Insert a transitional word or phrase to form a logical connection between ideas.**

Transition needed: Alex Haley spent many years researching the background for *Roots.*   Many critics believe *Roots* to be the most authentic work ever written about black Americans.

(A transitional phrase is needed to bridge the two ideas in the above sentences.)

Transition added: Alex Haley spent many years researching the background for *Roots.*   As a result, many critics believe *Roots* to be the most authentic work ever written about black Americans.

Var (variety)   **The marked passage needs more variety in sentence structure and length.**

Var   Many Americans with charge accounts are going bankrupt.   These consumers just can't control their spending habits.   They start off by buying small items on credit.   Then they purchase larger items.   Soon they are faced with high interest rates they can't pay.   Now they consolidate these small bills by taking out a major loan.   They now have one large bill they can't pay instead of having many small bills.   Thus they must declare bankruptcy.   Soon they start all over again.   It's the American way of life.

The sentences in the above passage lack variety. As a result, the passage is monotonous and fails to hold the reader's attention. The sentence structure should be varied and the overused pronoun *they* should be avoided.

Variety added:

For some consumers, charge accounts are an open invitation to bankruptcy. Many otherwise responsible Americans can't control their spending habits. They start by buying small items on credit. Then they purchase larger items. Soon the free-spending consumers are faced with high-interest payments on their credit accounts. To consolidate a number of separate burdens, a debtor may take out a major loan. Then, instead of having many small bills to pay, the consumer has one large bill but may still be unable to pay it. Sometimes the only way out of this never-ending cycle of payments is to declare bankruptcy and to start all over again. For all too many consumers, this is the American way of life.

Vb (*verb form*) **Change the marked verb to the correct form.**

All verbs have three principal parts: the present infinitive, the past tense, and the past participle.

Regular Verbs

The past tense and the past participle of regular verbs are formed by adding *d* or *ed* to the present infinitive.

Past Tense: We want*ed* to go to the park.
Past Participle: We had want*ed* to go to the park.
(Note: The past participle is always used with an auxiliary verb. "We *had* wanted to go to the park.")

Irregular Verbs

Many verbs are irregular in form. To find the principal parts of these verbs, you should consult a dictionary. If a verb is regular, only the present infinitive will be given. If a verb is irregular, the principal parts will be listed.

Some Irregular Verbs

INFINITIVE	PAST TENSE	PAST PARTICIPLE
begin	began	begun
blow	blew	blown
break	broke	broken
bring	brought	brought
come	came	come
do	did	done
drink	drank	drunk
eat	ate	eaten
freeze	froze	frozen
know	knew	known
see	saw	seen
write	wrote	written

Incorrect: He *seen* me last night.

(*Seen* is the past participle of the irregular verb *see*.   As noted earlier, the past participle is never used without an auxiliary verb.)

Correct: He had seen me last night.

Incorrect: She had *comed* to the party.

(The verb *come* is irregular and does *not* form its past participle by adding *ed*.)

Correct: She had come to the party.

¶ *(paragraph)*   **Start a new paragraph where marked.**

Note: A paragraph consists of sentences that develop one main idea. Usually, the paragraph begins with a topic sentence that clearly states the one idea to be discussed or explained.   A well-written paragraph never wanders away from the main idea expressed in its topic sentence.

A Model Paragraph

Topic Sentence   *Alcohol is an intoxicant that can be very dangerous in its effects.* When used in moderation, alcohol can ease tension and produce feelings of well-being.   Taken in excess, alcohol can have disastrous results.   Since alcohol acts as a depressant, the drinker's performance of the simplest tasks is impaired if too much alcohol is taken into the blood stream too rapidly.   Walking straight and talking clearly are problems, and more importantly, the reflexes needed to drive a car are slowed down.   As a result, drinking drivers are the major cause of highway accidents in the United States.   Furthermore, for certain individuals, alcohol can be physically and psychologically addictive.   Alcoholism is the fourth most prevalent disease in the United States, and it can lead to early death, as from cirrhosis of the liver.   Clearly, alcohol can be extremely dangerous in its effects.

No ¶(*no paragraph*)   **Do not begin a paragraph where marked.**

SECTION 3: HANDBOOK

PART ONE:

Review of Grammar and Usage

The sentence is the basic unit of expression in all types of writing. Any type of written expression, such as a report, newspaper article, textbook, message, or essay, is built upon the sentence.

This review is divided into three lessons. The first lesson is concerned with the *main* and *secondary elements* of the sentence. The second lesson discusses types of sentences: *simple, compound,* and *complex.* The third lesson concentrates on the most *common errors* students make when they write sentences. This third lesson depends upon the two lessons that come before it because an understanding of sentence elements and sentence types will help you to avoid making these common errors.

DEFINITION OF MAIN TERMS

1. **Adjective**—a word that modifies (changes, limits, describes) a noun or pronoun.

2. **Adverb**—a word that modifies a verb, adjective, adverb, or the whole sentence.

3. **Clause**—a group of words containing a subject and a predicate. See **Dependent Clause** and **Independent Clause.**

4. **Complement**—part of a sentence that completes the meaning of the verb.

5. **Complete Predicate**—everything in the sentence that is not the complete subject. The most important part of the predicate is the verb.

6. **Complete Subject**—the living being, place, thing, or idea being discussed in the sentence, along with its modifiers.

7. **Complex Sentence**—a sentence composed of an independent clause and one or more dependent clauses.

8. **Compound Sentence**—two or more independent clauses joined by a coordinating conjunction.

9. **Conjunction**—a word joining together whole sentences or parts of sentences.

10. **Dependent Clause**—a subject and a predicate that are introduced by a subordinating conjunction or relative pronoun and that *cannot* stand alone as a sentence.

11. **Independent Clause**—a subject and a predicate that *can* stand alone as a sentence.

12. **Linking Verb**—a verb that expresses a condition rather than a direct action.

13. **Main Elements of the Sentence**—the parts of the sentence that give you the basic information you need in order to read the sentence. The simple subject, verb, object, and complement are main elements.

14. **Noun**—the name of a living being, place, lifeless thing, or idea.

15. **Object**—the direct object receives the action of the verb; the indirect object is the receiver of the direct object. In the sentence "Throw me the ball," *ball* is the direct object and *me* is the indirect object.

16. **Phrase**—a secondary sentence element that does not have a subject or verb.

17. **Preposition**—a word connecting a noun or pronoun to another noun, pronoun, verb, or adjective to show a relationship.

18. **Pronoun**—a word used in place of a noun.

19. **Run-together Sentence**—two or more sentences written as one sentence.

20. **Secondary Elements of the Sentence**—the parts of the sentence that modify (present some additional information about) the main elements. Adjectives, adverbs, phrases, and clauses are secondary elements.

21. **Sentence**—a group of words that expresses a complete thought. A sentence begins with a capital letter and ends with a period, question mark, or exclamation point.

22. **Sentence Fragment**—an incomplete sentence.

23. **Simple Sentence**—a sentence of one clause in which the subject and/or the verb may be singular or may be compound.

24. **Verb**—a word that expresses an action or state of being, telling what the subject does, has, or is.

Lesson 1
The Elements of a Sentence

G1 **The Main Elements of the Sentence:**
SUBJECT, VERB, OBJECT, COMPLEMENT

The Subject and the Predicate

The COMPLETE SUBJECT *tells who* or *what* you are talking about. This *who* or *what* is usually a noun or a pronoun and the additional words that describe or limit its meaning. Another way to identify the complete subject is to look for the living being, place, thing, or idea being discussed, along with the words that describe or limit it. The SIMPLE SUBJECT is the living being, place, thing, or idea *without* the additional words.

Examples: The simple subjects (in these examples, always nouns) are underlined. The arrows indicate which word or words modify the nouns.

COMPLETE SUBJECT

My favorite <u>aunt</u>   came to visit.

The hungry <u>cat</u>   waited at the door.

<u>Tables</u> of gold   were on display.

Industrial <u>San Francisco</u>   has business opportunities.

<u>Freedom</u> without responsibility   is impossible.

<u>Helga</u>   is asleep.

156

Drill 1—Read the following sentences carefully. Underline the SIMPLE SUBJECT of the sentence. The first one is done for you.

1. Most <u>people</u> try to diet at one time or another.

2. Last year Bill Cannon weighed 341 pounds.

3. He seemed to be gaining weight daily.

4. He had tried every imaginable fad diet without success.

5. Now at 200 pounds, the man has a different image of himself.

6. His remarkable weight loss is due to steady, well-balanced dieting and exercise under a doctor's supervision.

7. Excessive weight is a common problem in today's society.

8. Years ago, fat people were thought to be wealthy people.

9. Only the rich had enough money to buy lots of food.

10. Now, however, fashionable and wealthy people want to be slim.

The COMPLETE PREDICATE tells what you are saying about the subject. The most important word in the PREDICATE is the verb. The verb tells what the subject does, has, or is.

Examples: The verbs are underlined, and the arrows indicate which words modify them.

COMPLETE SUBJECT	COMPLETE PREDICATE
The orchestra	<u>played</u> loudly.
We	<u>came</u> early.
The relatives	<u>are leaving</u> soon.
Jennifer	never <u>forgets</u> her homework.
I	<u>understand</u> that assignment easily.

The Verb

The VERB, which is the most important word (or word grouping) in the PREDICATE, is usually an action word. Sometimes the verb expresses the *action* of a sentence:

Example: It snowed last night.
 Snowed names the action of the sentence.
 Snowed is the VERB.

Often the VERB tells what the SUBJECT *does* or *has*:

Example: Juan plays football.
　　　　　　Plays tells what Juan does.
　　　　　　Plays is the VERB.

Example: The jar contains 300 marbles.
　　　　　　Contains tells that the jar has something.
　　　　　　Contains is the VERB.

Most VERBS are action words, but some VERBS tell that the SUBJECT *is* something.   These VERBS are called VERBS OF BE-ING.

Example: Maria is a good singer.
　　　　　　Is connects with a description of Maria.
　　　　　　Is is the VERB.

Along with *is*, all the forms of *be*, such as *are, was, were, has been,* and *will be,* are VERBS OF BEING.

The VERB is the one word in a sentence that changes form to indicate *a change of time.*

Example: I *ask* your opinion now.   (present)
　　　　　　I *asked* your opinion before.   (past)

Drill 2—Read the following sentences.   Indicate the verb in the space provided by writing in the one word that changes form to show a time change.   The first one is done for you.

1. Now I *am* in a good mood.
　　Before, I *was* in a good mood.　　　　　__am__ changed to __was__

2. Now I want to relax.
　　Before, I _____ to relax.　　　　　_____ changed to _____
　　　　　　fill in

3. Now, I like her.
　　Before, I _____ her.　　　　　_____ changed to _____
　　　　　　fill in

4. Now, I have money.
　　Before, I _____ money.　　　　　_____ changed to _____
　　　　　　fill in

5. Now, I am planning to go.
　　Before, I _____ planning to go.　　_____ changed to _____
　　　　　　fill in

158

Drill 3—Find the verb in the following sentences. Then write the verb in the space provided.

1. You dance beautifully.   1. _____

2. She is a good salesperson.   2. _____

3. Vivian believes in me.   3. _____

4. I bake bread in my spare time.   4. _____

5. Rebecca has a terrible cold.   5. _____

6. I was in a good mood.   6. _____

7. Carlos planned to go to the party.   7. _____

8. It rained all day yesterday.   8. _____

9. While running down the street,
   George fell down.   9. _____

10. The spring leaves unfurl slowly.   10. _____

Caution about Verbs:
Many VERBS are made up of more than one word.

Example: We *are eating* lunch now.

In this sentence, *are* and *eating* both make up the VERB of the sentence. *Eating* is the main part of the VERB, and *are* is the helping (auxiliary) VERB. Both words together tell what the SUBJECT does, but only the helping VERB changes to show a time change.

Example: We *were eating* lunch before.
           Are changes to *were*.

These verbs of more than one word can be a problem when the *ing* form (called the *verbal*) is confused with the VERB.

INCORRECT	CORRECT
He calling her.	He is calling her.

Note:
    This is incorrect because you must use a helping VERB in front of the verbal *calling*.

159

Another verbal form often mistaken for a verb is the *to* form, or infinitive.

INCORRECT	CORRECT
The boy to want the cake.	The boy wants the cake.

Note:
> This is incorrect because you must use a true VERB instead of the infinitive.

Drill 4—Put an X before the verb forms that cannot be used alone as a verb in a sentence.

1. ___ is   6. ___ are helping

2. ___ to be   7. ___ to go

3. ___ planning   8. ___ has found

4. ___ have   9. ___ investigating

5. ___ was   10. ___ were considering

The Object

There are two kinds of OBJECTS in a sentence.

The DIRECT OBJECT *receives the action* of the VERB or *shows the result* of the action.

Example: Jean hit the ball.
> *Hit* is the VERB.
> *Ball* is the DIRECT OBJECT.

The INDIRECT OBJECT is used with verbs of *asking, giving,* or *telling.* It names the receiver of the DIRECT OBJECT (the question, gift, or message).

Example: Larry sent Linda a telegram.
> *Telegram* is the DIRECT OBJECT of the VERB *sent.*
> *Linda* is the INDIRECT OBJECT of the VERB *sent.*
> *Linda* is the receiver of the DIRECT OBJECT—*telegram.*

Example: They asked the teacher a question.
> *Question* is the DIRECT OBJECT of the VERB *asked.*
> *Teacher* is the INDIRECT OBJECT of the VERB *asked.*
> *Teacher* is the receiver of the DIRECT OBJECT—*question.*

Example: Susan gave Andy a watch.
Watch is the DIRECT OBJECT of the VERB *gave*.
Andy is the INDIRECT OBJECT of the VERB *gave*.
Andy is the receiver of the DIRECT OBJECT—*watch*.

Complete Subject	Complete Predicate		
	Verb	**Indirect Object**	**Direct Object**
Larry	sent	Linda	a telegram
They	asked	the teacher	a question
Susan	gave	Andy	a watch

Drill 5—Some of the following sentences contain a DIRECT OB-JECT. Others have both a DIRECT OBJECT and an INDIRECT OBJECT. Put *D.O.* over each DIRECT OBJECT and *I.O.* over each INDIRECT OBJECT. The first one is done for you.

1. Ms. Simpson showed us her new camera.
                   I.O.   **D.O.**

2. Jason flew his kite.

3. Ann asked her teacher a question.

4. The mail carrier brought me a special delivery letter.

5. They watch television.

6. Julio told his little sister a bedtime story.

7. I sent Freda a message.

8. Sarah gave Mark a present.

9. She painted a picture for him.

10. Angelo lent me a dollar.

The Complement

Just as there are two kinds of OBJECTS, there are also two kinds of COMPLEMENTS. The SUBJECT COMPLEMENT follows a linking verb and tells something about the subject of the sentence.

Linking verbs are not complete in themselves. They link, or combine, two elements: the subject and the complement.

The most common linking verbs are all the forms of the verb *to be:* *is, are, was, were, been, will be,* etc. Other linking verbs are *become, appear, feel, seem, look, smell, sound,* and *taste.*

Example: Myrna is the student teacher.
The words *student teacher* complete the sentence and tell us something about Myrna.
You cannot say "Myrna is" (except merely to say that she exists); you must say *what* she is.
In this case, *student teacher* is the SUBJECT COMPLEMENT.

Example: Willy feels happy.
The word *happy* completes the sentence, telling us *how* Willy feels.
In this case, *happy* is the SUBJECT COMPLEMENT.

Just as the SUBJECT COMPLEMENT tells us about the SUBJECT, the OBJECT COMPLEMENT tells us about the DIRECT OBJECT of the sentence.

Example: The class elected Pat president.
Pat is the DIRECT OBJECT of the verb *elected.*
President is the OBJECT COMPLEMENT. It tells us something about Pat, the DIRECT OBJECT.
Example: The jury found the defendant guilty.
Defendant is the DIRECT OBJECT of the verb *found.*
Guilty is the OBJECT COMPLEMENT. It tells us something about the *defendant.*

Drill 6—Read the following sentences. Then put S.C. over each SUBJECT COMPLEMENT and O.C. over each OBJECT COMPLEMENT. The first one is done for you.

 O.C.
1. They elected Sandy class president.

2. The cake tasted delicious.

3. Pablo is becoming a teacher.

4. He considered his new job a success.

5. The candy kept the children quiet.

6. Kate will be famous soon.

7. The book kept me occupied.

8. They seem better now.

9. The soup tasted salty.

10. Darlene thought the movie a failure.

 ## The Secondary Elements of the Sentence: ADJECTIVES and ADVERBS

The main elements of the sentence are not usually enough to say everything you want to say. You need additional words or word groupings—SECONDARY ELEMENTS—to make the meaning of the main elements more precise. Adjectives, adverbs, and phrases and clauses that serve as modifiers are SECONDARY ELEMENTS.

The Adjective

An adjective *modifies* (describes or makes more precise the meaning of) a noun or pronoun.

Example: The new teacher is here.
           New modifies the noun *teacher,* describing the teacher.
           New is an *ADJECTIVE.*

Example: It was a silly and boring movie.
           Silly and *boring* modify the noun *movie.*
           Silly and *boring* are ADJECTIVES.

Drill 1—Place the abbreviation ADJ. over the ADJECTIVES contained in the following sentences. The first one is done for you.

                       adj.
  1. Susan is an excellent carpenter.

  2. Who is the tallest student in the class?

  3. A mysterious stranger sat near me in the restaurant.

  4. Sam's employer said that he was a good and reliable worker.

  5. Some self-serving politicians live by their own rules.

6. *Rebel Without a Cause* was a serious film.

7. You ask difficult and complex questions.

8. Gloria gave her attacker a sharp kick in the shin.

9. Lee tried to swim in the choppy water.

10. Chris gave a pink rose to Pat.

The Adverb

Now that we understand what an ADJECTIVE is, let us look at ADVERBS.

An ADVERB usually modifies a verb, adjective, or other adverb. But sometimes, an ADVERB can modify the sentence as a whole.

Example: I ran quickly.
     Quickly modifies the VERB *ran.*
     Quickly is an ADVERB.

Example: Ben felt very sad.
     Very modifies the ADJECTIVE *sad.*
     Very is an ADVERB.

Example: Jo swam quite well today.
     Quite modifies the ADVERB *well.*
     Quite is an ADVERB.

Example: Honestly, I feel exhausted.
     Honestly modifies the whole sentence.
     Honestly is an ADVERB.

Drill 2—Place the abbreviation ADV. over the ADVERBS contained in the following sentences.   The first one is done for you.

        adv.
1. They walked cautiously on the slippery sidewalk.

2. We plan to leave soon.

3. Lina smiled confidently when it was her turn to speak.

4. He is not feeling too well.

5. Robin is an extremely able student.

6. Sue and Bill Porter are very helpful neighbors.

7. They wash their car quite often.

8. Actually, I cannot help you.

9. Ken lovingly glanced at his newborn child.

10. The questions ranged from the very difficult to the extremely easy.

The Clause

As you have learned, the sentence is made up of main elements and secondary elements. A CLAUSE can be either a main element or a secondary element of a sentence.

The main clause, or INDEPENDENT CLAUSE, can be a complete sentence by itself, with a SUBJECT and a PREDICATE. It makes a complete statement.

SUBJECT	PREDICATE
I	went home.

The subordinate clause, or DEPENDENT CLAUSE, does not make a complete statement by itself. It is a *secondary* element of a sentence. It needs a subordinating conjunction or relative pronoun to connect it to the MAIN CLAUSE. For example, *because it was dark* is a DEPENDENT CLAUSE.

The word *because* indicates that something must come before or after the CLAUSE to complete it.

I went home because it was dark is a complete sentence. It has an INDEPENDENT CLAUSE, *I went home.* And it has a DEPENDENT CLAUSE, *because it was dark.*

Sometimes the DEPENDENT CLAUSE comes before the INDEPENDENT CLAUSE. *Because it was dark, I went home.*

The words which signal that a DEPENDENT CLAUSE is to follow are subordinating conjunctions and relative pronouns. The most common subordinating conjunctions are: *after, although, as, because, before, if, once, since, that, until, when, where, while.*

The relative pronouns are: *who, whom, whose, which, that.*

Drill 3—In the following sentences, underline the INDEPENDENT CLAUSE once and the DEPENDENT CLAUSE twice. Circle the subordinating conjunction or relative pronoun that introduces the DEPENDENT CLAUSE. The first one is done for you.

1. Jose could swim across the river (when) he was fourteen.

2. The road became rougher as we progressed.

3. When they saw the police officer coming toward them, the thieves ran away.

4. Gene is an excellent student, who will probably be a fine lawyer.

5. Before television was available, people read more books.

6. Heather worked on her car until her father called her.

7. Pete has a dog that is eighteen years old.

8. I sent Mother daisies, which are her favorite flowers.

9. Although it rained all day, we still had fun.

10. Adele has a cousin named Beth, who is studying medicine.

The Prepositional Phrase

The PHRASE is also a *secondary* sentence element which depends upon other sentence elements. It cannot make a sentence by itself, and it does not have a subject or a predicate.

These are PREPOSITIONAL PHRASES:

across the filthy street

at midnight

between the parked cars

with Juan and me

A PREPOSITIONAL PHRASE is made up of a PREPOSITION (such as *to, at, from, by, in, out, of, with, for, between, under,* or *across*) and the object of the PREPOSITION (along with possible modifiers). The object of the PREPOSITION is always a noun or pronoun.

The PREPOSITION relates the noun or pronoun to another word in the sentence.

Drill 4—Each of the following sentences contains a PREPOSITIONAL PHRASE. Underline the PREPOSITIONAL PHRASE. (Note that the first sentence has two PREPOSITIONAL PHRASES and the last sentence has four.) The first one is done for you.

1. Women who work <u>outside the home</u> are nothing new <u>in our society</u>.

2. However, the number of women holding paid employment has grown tremendously.

3. The back-to-work movement has been influenced by different social forces.

4. Limiting a job category to one sex or the other is now illegal.

5. Earlier in the century, the "technology of the kitchen" gave women time for paid work outside the home.

Review Exercise 1   Supplying the Main and Secondary Elements of the Sentence.

Each of the following items is missing one of the main or secondary elements of the sentence.

Example: _____ rode home after nine.
            A SUBJECT is needed before the verb *rode.* If we supply a
            name, *Ronald,* the complete sentence will read:
            <u>Ronald</u> rode home after nine.

Fill in the missing elements.

1. _____ found a wallet.
       SUBJECT

2. Jerry _____ the car.
           VERB

3. Chris gave Pat _____.
               DIRECT OBJECT

4. The scientist told _____ the secret formula.
               INDIRECT OBJECT

5. Robin appears _____ .
SUBJECT COMPLEMENT

6. The waiter made the customer _____ .
OBJECT COMPLEMENT

7. A _____ child asked me a question.
ADJECTIVE

8. The dog ate _____ .
ADVERB

9. Ruth _____ the test with a _____ mark.
VERB   ADJECTIVE

10. They danced _____ .
ADVERB

Review Exercise 2   Reviewing the Main and Secondary Elements of the Sentence.

The basic questions of *who, what, when, where,* and *how* will help you to understand the Main and Secondary Elements of the sentence. Read the following sentences. Answer the questions on the lines provided.

Example: George studies hard.

1. Who studies hard? SUBJECT _____George_____ .

2. What does he do? VERB _____studies_____ .

3. How does he study? ADVERB _____hard_____ .

A.   The cheering students elected Randy president.

1. Who elected Randy president?   SUBJECT _____

2. What did they do?   VERB _____

3. Whom did they elect?   DIRECT OBJECT _____

4. What did they elect Randy?

OBJECT COMPLEMENT _____

5. What kind of students were they?

ADJECTIVE _____

B. Arthur quickly made Lilly a sandwich.

  6. Who made Lilly a sandwich? SUBJECT _____

  7. What did Arthur do? VERB _____

  8. What did Arthur make? DIRECT OBJECT _____

  9. Whom did Arthur make the sandwich for?

  INDIRECT OBJECT _____

10. How did Arthur make the sandwich?

  ADVERB _____

C. Leslie hurriedly appointed Ramon captain.

11. Who appointed Ramon captain? SUBJECT _____

12. What did Leslie do? VERB _____

13. Whom did Leslie appoint? DIRECT OBJECT _____

14. What did Leslie appoint Ramon?

  OBJECT COMPLEMENT _____

15. How did Leslie appoint Ramon? ADVERB _____

D. Elise carefully handed Harry the camera.

16. Who handed Harry the camera? SUBJECT _____

17. What did Elise do? VERB _____

18. What did Elise hand Harry? DIRECT OBJECT _____

19. Who did Elise hand the camera to?

  INDIRECT OBJECT _____

20. How did Elise hand the camera? ADVERB _____

Lesson 2

Types of Sentences

 The Simple Sentence

An independent clause has a subject and predicate and makes a complete statement.

A SIMPLE SENTENCE also has a *subject* and *predicate* and makes a complete statement.

Example: Chris loves Pat.
Remember, a SIMPLE SENTENCE has one independent clause and no dependent (subordinate) clauses.

The subject of a SIMPLE SENTENCE can have more than one part.   In that case, we call it a compound subject.

Example: Angela and Rafael joined the hiking club.
Angela and Rafael: compound subject in a SIMPLE SENTENCE

The verb of a simple sentence can also have more than one part. We call this kind of verb a compound verb.

Example: Marie saw and heard the moving train.
saw and heard: compound verb in a SIMPLE SENTENCE

Both subject and verb can be compound.

Example: Sandra and her mother laughed and sang at the party.
Sandra and her mother: compound subject
laughed and sang: compound verb in a SIMPLE SENTENCE

Here are some patterns of SIMPLE SENTENCES:

1. SUBJECT   VERB
    We   slept.

2. SUBJECT   VERB   OBJECT
    Ed   ate   supper.

3. SUBJECT   VERB   SUBJECT-COMPLEMENT
    Sue   looks   happy.

4. SUBJECT + SUBJECT   VERB
    Bill and Terry   cried.

5. SUBJECT   VERB + VERB
    The doctor   listened and observed.

6. SUBJECT + SUBJECT   VERB + VERB   OBJECT
    The scientist and   planned and   the experiment.
    her assistant   prepared

Drill 1—Read each sentence. Then underline the elements that make the correct pattern. The first sentence is done for you. (Note in the first sentence that *complement* is not underlined because it is not part of the pattern.)

1. Chris kissed Pat.
    <u>SUBJECT</u> <u>VERB</u> COMPLEMENT <u>OBJECT</u>

2. Babies cry.
    SUBJECT VERB   OBJECT

3. The dog whined and howled.
    SUBJECT VERB + VERB INDIRECT OBJECT

4. Theresa and Pedro cleaned the gym.
    SUBJECT + SUBJECT VERB COMPLEMENT OBJECT

5. Frankie feels sick.
    SUBJECT + SUBJECT VERB SUBJECT-COMPLEMENT

6. May and her brother danced and sang in the show.
    SUBJECT + SUBJECT VERB + VERB

7. They elected him treasurer.
    SUBJECT VERB OBJECT OBJECT-COMPLEMENT

8. The winter wind feels cold.
 SUBJECT   VERB   OBJECT   SUBJECT-COMPLEMENT

9. Helaine was determined.
 SUBJECT   VERB   SUBJECT-COMPLEMENT

10. Jeff and Marcia love their dogs.
 SUBJECT + SUBJECT   VERB   COMPLEMENT   OBJECT

 G4   **The Complex Sentence**

The COMPLEX SENTENCE is a sentence made up of an independent clause and one or more dependent (subordinate) clauses.

By definition, the dependent clause cannot stand by itself. The word *dependent* means "unable to stand alone."

INDEPENDENT CLAUSE	DEPENDENT CLAUSE
The picnic will be postponed	if it rains.

The independent clause (*The picnic will be postponed*) gives the important information. It can stand alone.

The dependent clause (*if it rains*) makes the meaning of the independent clause clearer, or extends the thought in some way. In the sample sentence, "if it rains" (dependent clause) explains under what conditions "the picnic will be postponed" (independent clause). *If* is a subordinating conjunction. Subordinating conjunctions signal that a dependent clause is to follow. Here are some other subordinating conjunctions: *after, although, as, because, before, once, since, that, until, when, where, while.*

INDEPENDENT CLAUSE	DEPENDENT CLAUSE
Madeline is a good runner	who wins many races.

Here, the dependent clause begins with a relative pronoun, *who.* Relative pronouns can signal that a dependent clause is to follow. Here are some other relative pronouns: *whom, whose, which, that.*

Drill 1—In the following sentences, underline the independent clause once and the dependent clause twice. Circle the *subordinating conjunction* or *relative pronoun* that introduces the dependent clause. The first one is done for you.

1. Please lock the door (when) you leave.
2. Since Professor Danton is ill, the lecture has been cancelled.
3. I liked her very much after I got to know her.
4. Laura bought a motorcycle, while her brother preferred a bicycle.
5. Arson is a crime that is growing to epidemic proportions.
6. Bob does not plan to wait up for them since they will be home late.
7. Teresa watched while the TV was repaired.
8. This is the adviser who will tell you about college programs.
9. Andy and Melissa live in Los Angeles, which is the third largest city in the United States.
10. Mercedes complained to her neighbor whose television had been blaring all night.

G5   The Compound Sentence

A COMPOUND SENTENCE is a SENTENCE that results from the combination of two or more independent clauses. Each of the clauses in a COMPOUND SENTENCE is a complete thought and can stand by itself as a sentence.

Example: 1. Our cousins are visiting us.
              2. They will stay for three days.

Sentences 1 and 2 are two separate sentences. We can make them into one COMPOUND SENTENCE by inserting the word AND between them. Of course, the period that ends the first sentence and the capital letter starting the second sentence will also be eliminated.

Our cousins are visiting us, and they will stay for three days.

AND is a coordinating conjunction. When it functions as a coordinating conjunction, AND joins sentences of equal importance.

The coordinating conjunctions are:

and, but, or, for, so, yet, nor

The most common coordinating conjunctions are:

and, but, or

(And) means that you are adding information of equal importance in the second independent clause of the COMPOUND SENTENCE.

I am leaving, (and) Michael is leaving with me.

(But) means that the second independent clause of the COM-POUND SENTENCE is true in spite of what is claimed in the first clause.

The math test was hard, (but) Rose passed it with flying colors.

(Or) means that each independent clause in the COMPOUND SENTENCE offers an alternative to choose between.

We could go to the nine o'clock movies, or we could watch TV at home.

Drill 1—Read the following sentences and underline the two independent clauses. Then circle the coordinating conjunction joining the clauses. The first sentence is done for you.

1. <u>Allegra loves reading,</u> (but) <u>she also likes TV.</u>

2. Mario attends school, and he has a part-time job in the super-market.

3. Cal won't run for the office, nor will he serve if elected.

4. Susie and Steve can come over here, or we can all go to the movies.

5. The sky looks threatening, yet the weather report says it will be sunny today.

6. I wanted to meet Jess, but we never seemed able to find the time.

7. Jorge needed to concentrate, so he went to the library to study.

8. Angela worked hard in her English class, for she wanted to be a writer.

9. Reggie Jackson hit that ball, and he slammed a home run.

10. Jeannine's long hair is beautiful, but she wears it up when she works.

Review Exercise 1   Here is a capsule description of the three types of sentences: simple, compound, and complex.

Subject + Verb = *Simple Sentence*

Simple Sentence + $\begin{Bmatrix} and \\ or \\ but \end{Bmatrix}$ Coordinating Conjunction + Simple Sentence = *Compound Sentence*

Simple Sentence + $\begin{Bmatrix} although \\ since \\ because \end{Bmatrix}$ Subordinating Conjunction   or   or $\begin{Bmatrix} who \\ which \end{Bmatrix}$ Relative Pronoun   + Dependent Clause = *Complex Sentence*

In the blank to the right of each sentence, indicate which type of sentence it is.

Example: The children laughed. _____SIMPLE_____

1. Peggy wanted to come, but the weather was bad. _____

2. Are you coming? _____

3. Janet Thompson played golf while her husband Joe took a nap.

   _____

4. Nick can choose to work tomorrow, or he can take a vacation day.

   _____

5. I am going to bed because I am tired. _____

6. Esther is studying to become an accountant. _____

7. Roy and Lucy are taking the train next Wednesday. _____

8. The patient coughed and sneezed in the doctor's office. _____

9. Although Percell got one question wrong, he did well on the test.

   _____

10. Terry participates in class, but Tony daydreams. _____

Review Exercise 2   Each of the following items is part of a COMPOUND or COMPLEX sentence. Complete the sentence in your own words.

Example: She laughed _____.
              She laughed *when she heard his story.*

1. When the curtain went up, _____

2. He smiled sweetly, although _____

_____.

3. Did you know Coach Raymond, whose _____

_____.

4. Carol plays the guitar, but _____

_____.

5. School will be closed if _____

_____.

6. Last winter was cold, and _____

_____.

7. Terry could get a part-time job, or _____

_____.

8. Because we saved our money, _____

_____.

9. Even though I attend school, _____

_____.

10. I enjoy going to the movies, yet _____

_____.

Lesson 3

Major Sentence Errors

 Subject-Verb Agreement

SUBJECT-VERB Agreement refers to the number of beings, places, things, or ideas being talked about.

If there is a single SUBJECT, the VERB must be singular.

Singular means *one.*

If there is a plural SUBJECT, the VERB must be plural.

Plural means *more than one.*

Example: The runner *wants* to win.
We are speaking about *one* runner; therefore, *runner* is a singular subject. The VERB *wants* is also singular. *Wants* is the form of the verb that belongs with *runner.*

Example: The runners *want* to win.
In this sentence, *runners* is a plural SUBJECT. We are speaking about several runners. *Want* is the form of the verb which belongs with *runners.*

Your only real problem with SUBJECT-VERB agreement is the third person singular of the present tense. Third person refers to someone or something other than first person—I, we—and second person—you. Present tense refers to something happening *now.*

Examples: The bird sings.
Nell Baline paints.
That paper rips easily.
Sal is happy.

Note the *s* ending on the third person singular verb.

Drill 1—In each sentence below, a verb is underlined. Fill in the blank in the second sentence with the same verb used in the first sentence, but change the form of the verb to go with the new subject. Use only the present tense. The first one is done for you.

1. **a.** The announcers (they) <u>report</u> the news.
   b. The announcer (he or she) <u>reports</u> the news.

2. **a.** The star reporters <u>make</u> the program a winner.
   b. The star reporter _____ the program a winner.

3. **a.** Their dark suits <u>are</u> not very attractive.
   b. His dark suit _____ not very attractive.

4. **a.** The baseball fans <u>cheer</u> for the home team.
   b. The baseball fan _____ for the home team.

5. **a.** The street musicians <u>play</u> good music.
   b. The street musician _____ good music.

6. **a.** The weather forecasters <u>show</u> the weather maps to us.
   b. The weather forecaster _____ the weather map to us.

7. **a.** The critics <u>review</u> the program.
   b. The critic _____ the program.

8. **a.** The schedules <u>are</u> very convenient.
   b. The schedule _____ very convenient.

9. **a.** The TV channels <u>have</u> a loyal group of viewers.
   b. The TV channel _____ a loyal group of viewers.

10. **a.** The reporters <u>have</u> a large audience.
    b. The reporter _____ a large audience.

Reminder: Subject-Verb Agreement with Compound Subjects

In our discussion of the SIMPLE SENTENCE, we introduced the COMPOUND SUBJECT. A subject made up of two or more parts joined by *and* is a compound subject.

Compound subjects take a plural VERB.

Example: Mark and Jonetta *watch* television.
George and his friends *like* jogging.

Many indefinite pronouns take a singular verb. *Everyone, everybody, no one, nobody, someone, somebody,* and *each* are examples of indefinite pronouns that require a verb which ends in *s.*

Example: Almost everybody *likes* to watch television.

Drill 2—Fill in the correct form of the verb *like* in the following sentences.

1. Anyone ——————— to watch television.

2. Everyone ——————— to watch television.

3. No one ——————— to watch television.

4. Someone ——————— to watch television.

5. Each person ——————— to watch television.

6. Neither ——————— to watch television.

7. Every person ——————— to watch television.

8. Everybody ——————— to watch television.

9. Somebody ——————— to watch television.

10. Nobody ——————— to watch television.

Sometimes a sentence begins with a word that appears to be the subject of the sentence but is not the subject. *Here* and *there* when followed by *is* or *are* are called *expletives*. Some people call such words ANTICIPATING SUBJECTS. When you see a sentence beginning with *here is* or *there are*, for example, you must look further to find the real subject of the sentence.

Example: There are many violent shows on television Tuesday night.
In this sentence, *there* is the ANTICIPATING SUBJECT.
The real subject is *shows* (plural).
The verb is *are* (plural).

Example: There is a violent show on television Tuesday night.
In this sentence, *there* is the ANTICIPATING SUBJECT.
The real subject is *show* (singular).
The verb is *is* (singular).

Drill 3—In the following sentences, underline the real subject. Then write the verb in the blank space. Use only the present tense of the verb *to be: is* with a singular subject and *are* with a plural subject. The first one is done for you.

1. There is one good television <u>program</u> on tonight.

2. There ——————— two good television programs on tonight.

3. Here ——————— a good television program to watch.

179

4. There _____ many blossoms on the tree now.

5. There _____ just one blossom on the tree.

6. Here _____ the winner of the award.

7. Here _____ the six winners of the awards.

8. There _____ a box of jewels.

9. Here _____ the site of many automobile accidents.

10. Here _____ some good television programs to watch.

Sometimes a prepositional phrase, such as *in the city,* comes between the subject and the verb. Occasionally, a dependent clause introduced by a relative pronoun will also come between the subject and verb. Neither affects the agreement of the main subject and verb.

                sub.   **prep. phrase** **verb**
Example: The *stores* (in the city) *are* large.

                sub.   **relative pronoun clause**
Example: That *tree* (which the electric company wants to chop down)
           verb
          is one hundred years old.

Drill 4—Write the present tense of the verb *to be* in the blank space: *is* with a singular subject and *are* with a plural subject. The first one is done for you.

1. The *star* on the program *is* my favorite performer.

2. The stars on the program _____ my favorite performers.

3. A commercial that comes at an exciting moment _____ very distracting.

4. That commercial between the programs _____ very distracting.

5. The neighbors across the street _____ nice.

6. The singer who is in the show _____ very talented.

7. The singers who are in the show ———————— very talented.

8. The actor who is in the series ———————— very talented.

9. The program that is on tonight ———————— my favorite.

10. The programs that are on tonight ———————— my favorites.

G7 The Sentence Fragment

In everyday language, we call a thing a fragment if it is broken off from something or is incomplete.   A sentence fragment is also a part of something—not a whole in itself.   When you read a sentence fragment, you are aware that it is incomplete and that more words are needed to express a complete thought.

Examples of Sentence Fragments:

    1. The red door

    2. prepared dinner

    3. was happy

These are complete sentences:

COMPLETE SUBJECT	COMPLETE PREDICATE
1. The red door	opened mysteriously.
2. Uncle Jim	prepared dinner.
3. Julio	was happy.

The Dependent Clause Fragment

Very often students confuse dependent clauses with sentences. However, a dependent clause is always a SENTENCE FRAGMENT.

A subordinating conjunction indicates that the group of words it introduces is not complete.

Examples of Sentence Fragments:

    When I came home . . .

    Because he telephoned . . .

    Although she knew it . . .

You need an independent clause to explain the assertion made in the dependent (subordinate) clause.

These are complete sentences:

DEPENDENT CLAUSE	INDEPENDENT CLAUSE
1. When I came home,	the electricity was out.
2. Because he telephoned,	we did not write to him.
3. Although she knew it,	Vanessa did not tell me the secret.

To correct sentence fragments:

1. Make sure that there is a subject and a verb and that the words express a complete thought.

2. If the fragment is lacking a subject or a verb, add what is necessary to make a complete sentence.

3. If the item is a dependent (subordinate) clause, add an independent clause.

Drill 1—Some of the items below are complete sentences. The others are not, either because they lack a subject or a verb or because they are introduced by a subordinating conjunction. (Remember, a subordinating conjunction indicates that the group of words it introduces is not a complete sentence.) The first item is done for you.

1. Although two people may be in love

Is this a complete sentence? __No__

If not, rewrite it: _Although two people may be in love, love alone will not ensure a successful marriage._

2. Young marriages are becoming more common

Is this a complete sentence? _____

If not, rewrite it: _____

3. Because young marriages are becoming more common today

Is this a complete sentence? _____

If not, rewrite it: _____

_____

_____

4. People want to be independent early in life

Is this a complete sentence? _____

If not, rewrite it: _____

_____

_____

5. When people want to be independent

Is this a complete sentence? _____

If not, rewrite it: _____

_____

_____

6. Since divorces are much more common today

Is this a complete sentence? _____

If not, rewrite it: _____

_____

_____

7. Plans have to be made carefully

Is this a complete sentence? _____

If not, rewrite it: _____

_____

_____

8. To make the right decision

Is this a complete sentence? _____

If not, rewrite it: _____

_____

_____

9. A place to live and money to spend

Is this a complete sentence? _____

If not, rewrite it: _____

_____

_____

10. After the wedding is over

Is this a complete sentence? _____

If not, rewrite it: _____

_____

_____

Drill 2—Read each three-line item and decide if there is an error that causes a sentence fragment. If so, note the letter beside the line in which the error occurs. Then check the letter for that line in the space provided on the right side of this sheet. If there is no error in all three lines, check the *O* space. The first one is done for you.

1. A Because young love seems glamorous. Many
    B young people are eager to fall in love
    C and then to get married right away.

1. A _x_ B__ C__ O__

2. A Television commercials often make young
    B people in love seem glamorous and happy.
    C The lovers always look joyfully carefree.

2. A __ B__ C__ O__

3. A The glamour of young love is "sold" on
    B television along with many products.
    C Such as cars, cosmetics, and dog food.

3. A__ B__ C__ O__

4. A Almost without fail each evening, at least
    B one television commercial shows the familiar
    C scene. Of two young lovers holding hands.

4. A__ B__ C__ O__

5. A Experienced television viewers know what to
B expect. When an ad's music is romantic. A
C product is being associated with love.

5. A__ B__ C__ O__

6. A I sometimes think about my
B childhood. Which was very pleasant.
C I had a lot of fun with friends.

6. A__ B__ C__ O__

7. A We used to jump rope often.
B We got our exercise this way.
C An easy way to get exercise.

7. A__ B__ C__ O__

8. A Children often get more exercise
B than adults do. Children are
C naturally more active and energetic.

8. A__ B__ C__ O__

9. A A three-year-old child seems to run
B nonstop. Around the house. An
C adult can hardly keep up with the child.

9. A__ B__ C__ O__

10. A Although exercise contributes to good health. Most adults do not
B get enough exercise. Since they lack
C exercise, they are often overweight.

10. A__ B__ C__ O__

 The Run-Together Sentence

A sentence fragment is incomplete. A RUN-TOGETHER sentence (sometimes called a RUN-ON sentence) is more than complete. It is usually two sentences that are written together without punctuation or with incorrect punctuation.

Example of a run-together sentence with no punctuation:
Marie explained the assignment Al understood it.

Examples of run-together sentences with incorrect punctuation:
Marie explained the assignment, Al understood it.
Marie explained the assignment, therefore, Al understood it.

To correct a run-together sentence:

1. Make it into separate sentences or independent clauses by using proper punctuation.
   Marie explained the assignment. Al understood it.
   Marie explained the assignment; therefore, Al understood it.

2. Make it into a compound sentence by using a coordinating conjunction.
   Marie explained the assignment, and Al understood it.

3. Make it into a complex sentence by using a subordinating conjunction.
   After Marie explained the assignment, Al understood it.
   Marie explained the assignment until Al understood it.

Drill 1—Here are some RUN-TOGETHER sentences. You can use the three recommended ways to correct each sentence: using proper punctuation, using a coordinating conjunction, or using a subordinating conjunction.

Example: He needed money for college therefore he took a part-time job.

Corrected with punctuation: He needed money for college. Therefore, he took a part-time job. *or* He needed money for college; therefore, he took a part-time job.

Corrected with a coordinating conjunction: He needed money for college, and therefore he took a part-time job.

Corrected with a subordinating conjunction: Because he needed money for college, he took a part-time job. (Note: In this case, the transition word *therefore* must be left out.)

1. Alfredo and Anna Maria wanted to get married, however they did not have their parents' permission.
   Correct with punctuation: _____

   _____

   Correct with a coordinating conjunction (*however* will be eliminated): _____

   _____

   Correct with a subordinating conjunction (*however* will be eliminated): _____

2. They were in love therefore the priest performed the marriage.

Correct with punctuation: _____

_____

Correct with a coordinating conjunction: _____

_____

Correct with a subordinating conjunction (*therefore* will be eliminated): _____

_____

3. They were married then they spent the night together.

Correct with punctuation: _____

_____

Correct with a coordinating conjunction: _____

_____

Correct with a subordinating conjunction: _____

_____

4. Alfredo had to leave Anna Maria the next morning, he was forced
to leave town to lead his gang in a fight.

Correct with punctuation: _____

_____

Correct with a coordinating conjunction (try the coordinating

conjunction *for*): _____

_____

Correct with a subordinating conjunction: _____

_____

5. Anna Maria's family argued with her all day, she was up worrying most of the night.

Correct with punctuation: _____

_____

Correct with a coordinating conjunction: _____

_____

Correct with a subordinating conjunction: _____

_____

6. Alfredo returned as quickly as he could, he found Anna Maria sound asleep.

Correct with punctuation: _____

_____

Correct with a coordinating conjunction: _____

_____

Correct with a subordinating conjunction: _____

_____

7. Anna Maria woke up she saw Alfredo smiling at her.

Correct with punctuation: _____

_____

Correct with a coordinating conjunction: _____

_____

Correct with a subordinating conjunction: _____

_____

8. Anna Maria told Alfredo he must go to the police, he was not convinced he should go.

Correct with punctuation: _____

_____

Correct with a coordinating conjunction: _____

_____

Correct with a subordinating conjunction: _____

_____

9. Fortunately a social worker was able to straighten out the situation, Alfredo and Anna Maria were able to stay together.

Correct with punctuation: _____

_____

Correct with a coordinating conjunction: _____

_____

Correct with a subordinating conjunction (try eliminating *fortunately):*

_____

10. This story has a happy ending everything does not always end happily in real life.

Correct with punctuation: _____

_____

Correct with a coordinating conjunction: _____

_____

Correct with a subordinating conjunction: _____

_____

G9   The Principal Parts of the Verb

A verb changes form to indicate a time change. Every verb can be written in four basic forms.

to walk

walk
(present)

walking
(present participle)

walked
(simple past)

walked
(past participle)

Even though the simple past and the past participle look the same in regular verbs, they are not used the same way.

The *simple past* is the form used to discuss an action that happened in the past.

> I *walked* home yesterday.

The *past participle* is the form used with a helping verb to discuss an action that was completed in the past before something else happened.

> I *had walked* home from school with Elaine until she moved away.

The past participle is also used with a helping verb to discuss an action that started in the past and has a continued effect in the present.

> I *have walked* home from school with Elaine for five years.

Most verbs in English are considered to be "regular." This means that the SIMPLE PAST and the PAST PARTICIPLE are both formed merely by adding *d* or *ed* to the simple present. There is no difference between the simple past and the past participle in regular verbs. Note the principal parts of the selected list of regular verbs below.

SIMPLE PRESENT	PRESENT PARTICIPLE (The *ING* form: always use with helping verbs such as: *am, are, is, was, were, will be.*)	SIMPLE PAST	PAST PARTICIPLE (Always use with helping verbs such as: *had, have, has, will have.*)
talk	talking	talked	talked
suggest	suggesting	suggested	suggested
develop	developing	developed	developed
drop	dropping	dropped	dropped
ship	shipping	shipped	shipped
love	loving	loved	loved
charge	charging	charged	charged
study	studying	studied	studied
worry	worrying	worried	worried

Drill 1—Fill in the blanks.

Simple Present	Present Participle	Simple Past	Past Participle
1. live	_____	_____	_____
2. _____	discovering	_____	_____
3. _____	_____	laughed	_____
4. beg	_____	_____	_____
5. _____	stopping	_____	_____
6. save	_____	_____	_____
7. _____	yelling	_____	_____
8. _____	_____	_____	believed
9. _____	_____	asked	_____
10. _____	carrying	_____	_____

English also has many verbs considered to be "irregular." An irregular verb does not follow a consistent pattern. Note the principal parts of the selected list of irregular verbs below.

SOME IRREGULAR VERBS

SIMPLE PRESENT	PRESENT PARTICIPLE (The *ING* form: always use with helping verbs such as: *am, are, is, was, were, will be.*)	SIMPLE PAST	PAST PARTICIPLE (Always use with helping verbs such as: *had, have, has, will have.*)
eat	eating	ate	eaten
break	breaking	broke	broken
steal	stealing	stole	stolen
see	seeing	saw	seen
grow	growing	grew	grown
do	doing	did	done
go	going	went	gone
am/are/is	being	was/were	been
drink	drinking	drank	drunk
bring	bringing	brought	brought
run	running	ran	run
sit	sitting	sat	sat
begin	beginning	began	begun
have/has	having	had	had
come	coming	came	come
give	giving	gave	given
write	writing	wrote	written

Drill 2—In the sentences below, circle the correct principal parts of the verb. The first one is done for you.

                              (broken)
1. A recent supersonic jet flight has broke speed records.

    come
2. Ford came into office because the former president resigned.

      seen
3. The observer saw the eclipse of the moon through a filter.

        written
4. The union officials have wrote a full account of their complaints.

went
5. The senators gone on a fact-finding trip to China.

given
6. The committee has gave her the art award.

did
7. They agreed that she had done a splendid job.

ate
8. I never have eaten so much in my life.

ran
9. Roger run the mile in exactly four minutes.

stole
10. The stopwatch was stolen from my locker.

Drill 3—Read each group of three lines below. If you find an error in the verb, check the letter for that line in the space provided on the right side of this sheet. If there is no error, check the *O* space. The first one is done for you.

1. A The entire family eaten all   **1.** A_×_ B__ C__ O__
   B the canned food that was later
   C found to contain botulism.

2. A The machine   **2.** A__ B__ C__ O__
   B run for more
   C than two hours.

3. A The treaty has brought   **3.** A__ B__ C__ O__
   B an end to the fighting
   C between the two countries.

4. A The television program   **4.** A__ B__ C__ O__
   B had began fifteen minutes
   C before the mayor arrived.

5. A The witness was able to give   **5.** A__ B__ C__ O__
   B the police many details about
   C the supermarket robbery he seen.

6. A The student had wrote   **6.** A__ B__ C__ O__
   B an excellent expository
   C essay about old age.

7. A The new fertilizer was so effective   **7.** A__ B__ C__ O__
   B that the houseplants has grow larger
   C than anyone thought possible.

8. A Thieves had stolen the   **8.** A__ B__ C__ O__
   B jewels before anyone
   C saw what was happening.

9. A The visitors had
   B arrived before the
   C monsoon rains came.

9. A__ B__ C__ O__

10. A Betty had done her
   B report while her sister
   C plays the radio.

10. A__ B__ C__ O__

G10 The Case of Pronouns

Pronouns cause difficulties because they change form in accordance with their use in the sentence.

Pronouns have three forms:

Subjective Case: *I, he, she, we, they, who*

Used in the sentence as:

1. subject of a verb: *She* went to the bank.

2. in apposition to the subject: We, Ken and *I*, washed the car.

3. predicate nominative: It is *I*.

Possessive Case: *my, mine, your, yours, her, hers, his, its, our, ours, their, theirs, everyone's, somebody's*

Used in the sentence as:

1. a word denoting possession: This is *my* book, not *yours*.   The book is *mine*.

2. a word that modifies a verbal (gerund): They appreciated *my* going to the store for them.

Objective Case: *me, her, him, us, them*

Used in the sentence as:

1. an object of the verb, infinitive, or preposition: I gave *him* the book.

2. an appositive to an object: She kissed us, Tom and *me*, at the door.

Note: The pronouns *it* and *you* are the same in the subjective and objective cases.   In the possessive case, the forms are *its* and *your* or *yours*.

Now let us look at some of the major writing errors that involve troublesome pronouns.

Problems Involving the Subjective Case

1. *Pronouns used as subject of the verb:* The pronoun indicates the person or thing acting. One rarely has trouble if the subject is singular. For example, we all know to say *I studied all weekend* instead of *Me studied all weekend.* The difficulty comes when the subject is compound:

> She and *I* (not me) studied all weekend.
>
> Larry and *she* (not her) will wash the dishes.

The point to remember is that whether the pronoun is used alone as a singular subject or as part of a compound subject, it must always be in the subjective case.

2. *Pronouns used in apposition to the subject:* When the pronoun is in close association with the subject, use the subjective case. Notice how *we* is closely associated with the subject *Democrats* in the following sentence:

> *We* (not us) Democrats must vote as one.

3. *Pronouns used as a predicate nominative:* When the pronoun means the same person or thing as the subject and is placed after the linking verb *to be,* use the subjective case:

> It was *he* (not him) who threw the ball.
>
> They announced that the winner of the scholarship was *she* (not her).

Problems Involving the Possessive Case

1. *Pronouns used to denote ownership—mine, yours, hers, his, theirs, its*—are not to be confused with pronouns that contain an apostrophe: *you're* (you are), *it's* (it is), *they're* (they are). These are simply pronouns with a contracted form of a *verb.*

> The dog ate its (*not* it's) bone.
>
> She put your (*not* you're) book on the desk.

2. *Pronouns that modify a verbal (gerund):*

> We admired *his* (not him) working so hard for the fund-raising drive.
>
> The director praised *their* (not them) dancing in the final act.

195

Problems Involving the Objective Case

1. *Pronouns used as an object of the verb, infinitive, or preposition:*

v. obj. v. obj.
She congratulated *him* (not he), then thanked *them* (not they).

inf. obj.
The winner turned out to be *me* (not I).

prep. obj.
They will divide the cake between you and *me* (not I).

prep. obj.
It was meant for you and *me* (not I).

Drill 1—In the following sentences, select the correct pronoun.

1. Jo and (I, me) are going to the basketball game.
2. (Us, We) seniors will play against the juniors.
3. She replied that it was (her, she) who was talking on the phone.
4. (Your, You're) composition is due tomorrow.
5. The lawyer objected to (him, his) leading the witness.
6. They woke (him, he) before dawn.
7. Henry said to find (she, her) before it was too late.
8. Between you and (I, me), he is the one at fault.
9. You are taller than either (she, her) or (I, me).
10. Alicia wondered about (their, them) going to college.

Review Exercise   Directions: In each of the following 15 questions, choose the letter of the CORRECT sentence and note it on your answer sheet. If there is no sentence that you think is correct, note *e* on your answer sheet.

1. a. Angelo missed the class, he had to get the notes of the lecture from Carlos.
  b. Julian whispered to Martha, he was bored with the work.
  c. The students attended a play in the Village, they enjoyed it very much.
  d. Cynthia had great love and respect for her parents, she tried to follow their advice in the situation.
  e. None of the above.

2. a. Tom asked Elizabeth for a ride, however, she was not going.

   b. It seems that the counseling staff is readily available, consequently many students seek their help.

   c. Ed had trouble living with his father and five younger brothers therefore he got his own apartment.

   d. The vendors on the corner were selling umbrellas all afternoon, nevertheless the police forced them to leave.

   e. None of the above.

3. a. The museum is offering a one-artist show of her paintings and sculpture, that is the first time she has received such high recognition for her work.

   b. I subscribe to three magazines this is very costly.

   c. The nurse was very polite Joyce cancelled her appointment.

   d. Don had one cigarette left in the apartment, but he was determined not to buy another pack.

   e. None of the above.

4. a. On the third floor.

   b. From every nook and cranny of the old house.

   c. In the cool of the evening.

   d. In sympathy to him.

   e. None of the above.

5. a. I was proud to be introduced to Ben Edwards. The champion chess player.

   b. There are certain things that I feel are necessary for clean living. Such as soap, water, and deodorant.

   c. They were given a choice of three electives. Principles of Economics, Economics of Developing Nations, Labor Economics.

   d. Florence Hansen, president of the Student Council, was present at the crucial meeting.

   e. None of the above.

6. a. Tim having missed the bus and deciding to walk twenty-five blocks.

   b. Emily Dickinson being considered one of the finest writers.

   c. Trying every alternative.

   d. If you listen to her, her arguments are logical.

   e. None of the above.

7. **a.** He treasured that book until the day it was stolen.

   b. Friends retrieved him from the water, and when he been awaked he realized what had happened.

   c. Emotion should not be disguise or kept in.

   d. Finally the man got disgusted and decide that it was time to move on, so he left town.

   e. None of the above.

8. **a.** He brung the book every day.

   b. Bertina and Leroy gone to the movies last night.

   c. Grace had bought the tickets and she given them to Sam.

   d. He had gotten ill the morning of the accounting exam.

   e. None of the above.

9. **a.** He seen the book on the table in the kitchen.

   b. Brenda been ill for the past week, and the discussion was difficult for her to follow.

   c. Alice led the class in a discussion of the three central symbols in the novel.

   d. Floyd could not have forgave Sandra for the lie which she told.

   e. None of the above.

10. **a.** The old movies that are on television late at night are the best.

    b. Every one of the assignments for this course are difficult.

    c. Salt, onions, and ketchup is my usual seasonings for a hamburger.

    d. Those who know her likes her.

    e. None of the above.

11. **a.** There are several good reasons for his leaving town.

    b. José and Elena is going to Puerto Rico.

    c. The apple crop are a big success this year.

    d. Ninety percent of the test were difficult for him.

    e. None of the above.

12. **a.** His clothes is very gaudy.

    b. The movie theater and the restaurant is on this block.

    c. Each of the classrooms have blackboards.

    d. Her new car and her new job was the best things in her life.

    e. None of the above.

13. a. She and I have been friends since first grade.

   b. Us boys may purchase the hubcaps and tires separately if we are interested in saving money.

   c. Him and I were in the same class.

   d. The student council elected she and I.

   e. None of the above.

14. a. We Americans have been very fortunate.

   b. It was her who answered the phone.

   c. Between you and I, Shirley Green is the candidate I would choose.

   d. Them in the business program and us in the liberal arts program met in the student lounge.

   e. None of the above.

15. a. Larry and her went to the party.

   b. Is Janice coming to you're party?

   c. The coach appreciated me making the winning point.

   d. Ann, Michael, and us had passed the history exam.

   e. None of the above.

PART TWO:

Punctuation, Mechanics, and Spelling

Although punctuation, mechanics, and spelling are details, they are important. An essay with no errors in punctuation, mechanics, or spelling is easier to read, allowing your audience to concentrate on what you are trying to say. Just as good manners ease relationships between people, correct punctuation, mechanics, and spelling are also courtesies that increase understanding between writer and reader. We are concerned here not with definitive sections on punctuation, mechanics, and spelling but rather with eliminating common errors that beginning writers often make.

Lesson 1
Punctuation

The marks of punctuation are aids to reading and writing. In this lesson, we will concentrate only on those marks of punctuation that prove at times to be troublesome. Study the way punctuation is employed here if you wish to solve your problems.

 The Period .

The PERIOD marks the end of a sentence.

Example: David is waiting downstairs.

You will remember that a PERIOD can be used to correct a RUN-TOGETHER sentence. Putting a period at the end of the first sentence and capitalizing the first word of the second sentence will convert the RUN-TOGETHER sentence into two separate sentences.

Incorrect:

Denise called to her brother he was playing in the yard.

Tony went to the city, Louise went to the beach.

Correct:

Denise called to her brother. He was playing in the yard.

Tony went to the city. Louise went to the beach.

The PERIOD is used after initials and after most abbreviations.

Examples: Susan B. Anthony   O. J. Simpson   A.D.   B.C.
B.A.   Mr.   Ms.   N.Y.   L.A.   Ave.

The four main uses of the period are:

1. to end a sentence

2. to correct run-together sentences

3. to mark initials

4. to mark abbreviations

Drill 1—Read the following sentences. Place a period wherever you think one is needed. Sometimes you may have to change a small letter to a capital. The first sentence is done for you.

1. Lucy called Brad to the telephone. The stereo was too loud for him to hear her.
2. Today is the first day of spring
3. Please address the envelope as follows: 16 Main St, Dobbs Ferry, N Y 10522
4. When you graduate from college, you will receive a B A or B S degree
5. The children were laughing and singing, they were having a good time
6. Toby S T Denton signed the register, but he forgot to put down that he is from Washington, D C
7. The sun was shining and the sky was blue, we decided to go to the beach.
8. Mr. Herman L R Jones worked for six years to obtain his M D
9. Ernest never seems to have time to do his homework he is so busy
10. Ms S R Peters was offered a good job, she had an M A degree in history

 The Comma ,

The COMMA has four main purposes:

1. to separate
2. to enclose
3. to introduce
4. to show omission

In this book, we will concentrate on the two purposes of the COMMA that are misunderstood by many students: the COMMA that is used *to separate* certain elements of a sentence and then the COMMA as it is used *to enclose* certain elements of the sentence.

The COMMA is used to *separate* certain elements of the sentence.

1. In a compound sentence, independent clauses are connected by a coordinating conjunction. A COMMA is placed before the coordinating conjunction to separate the two independent clauses.

    Example: Lola had made plans to study, but Ramon persuaded her to go to the movies.

2. When a dependent clause is joined to an independent clause, it makes a complex sentence. If the dependent clause comes at the beginning of the complex sentence, the COMMA separates the dependent clause from the independent clause.

    Example: Although it was 2 A.M., Salena was determined to finish the essay she was writing.

3. When a long phrase is introductory, a COMMA separates it from the rest of the sentence.

    Example: In the early hours of the morning, Mark would attempt to write his composition.

4. The COMMA separates items in a series. (Note: The comma before *and* is optional.)

    Example: We will need mustard, ketchup, pickles, relish, and salt for the picnic.

5. The COMMA separates items to prevent confusion or misreading.

    Incorrect: In my home work is emphasized.

    Correct: In my home, work is emphasized.

    (Here the two words *home* and *work* are separated to avoid confusion with the word *homework.*)

The COMMA is used to *enclose* certain elements of the sentence.

6. The COMMA is used to enclose those modifiers that are not essential to the meaning of the sentence. If the modifiers are essential to a sentence, you must not enclose them in commas.

    Example: His immediate family, his mother and father, will be at the graduation.

The words *his mother and father* mean the same thing as *his immediate family*. Thus the words *his mother and father* are not essential and must be enclosed in commas.

> Example: The students who play basketball will not be able to use the gym during the exhibit.

Here the words *who play basketball* are necessary to make clear who the students are. Therefore, the words are essential to the sentence and should not be enclosed in commas.

Remember, the uses of the COMMA are:

1. to separate two independent clauses
2. to separate dependent from independent clauses
3. to separate a long introductory phrase from the rest of the sentence
4. to separate items in a series
5. to separate confusing items
6. to enclose nonessential modifiers

Drill 2—Read the following sentences. Place a comma wherever you think one is needed. The first sentence is done for you.

1. Odette ordered a pizza with a special topping, mushrooms and peppers, for her friends.
2. My father is playing cards with Uncle Jim Duke Dixie and Ruby.
3. Her aunt told Nerissa to buy milk eggs and bread at the store.
4. She bought the latest record of her favorite group Pink Floyd when it was on sale.
5. Filbert asked me to dance but I really wanted to dance with Harry.
6. After the concert had ended Keith still wanted to hear more.
7. We had known Joan a champion swimmer for nine years.
8. Last night I bought a new jacket and an old tailor lengthened the sleeves for me.
9. He tried out for the baseball football basketball and track teams.
10. On the bus in the afternoon she tried to finish her homework.

P3   The Semicolon ;

The SEMICOLON may be used in place of coordinating conjunctions to separate the independent clauses in a compound sentence.

Example: The teacher lectured; the students listened.

The SEMICOLON is used between independent clauses joined by transitional (connective or linking) words, such as *however, thus, therefore, nevertheless,* or *then.*

Example: It rained all day; therefore, we did not go to the beach.

The SEMICOLON separates coordinate elements in a series when the items in the series contain subdivisions.

Example: I would love to visit Edinburgh, Scotland; Nice, France; and Jerusalem, Israel.

When there is no subdivision in the series, use only commas.

Example: I would love to visit Scotland, France, and Israel.

The three main uses of the SEMICOLON are:

1. to separate independent clauses not joined by coordinating conjunctions
2. to separate independent clauses joined by certain transitional words
3. to separate items in a series when the items are already subdivided

Drill 3—Read the sentences below.   Place a semicolon wherever you think one is needed.   To do so, you may have to eliminate some commas.   The first sentence is done for you.

1. Potholes in the streets are dangerous; the city ought to fix them.
2. The rain is slowing down, however, it hasn't stopped yet.
3. My three favorite places are Barcelona, Spain, Rome, Italy, and Kansas City, Missouri.
4. I am so hungry, breakfast was four hours ago.

5. Gail could not sing very well nevertheless, she tried hard.

6. Among those present were Dr. Madeline T. Harrow, New York City Community College Dr. Paul J. Cartney, London School of Economics and Dr. Jean-Jacques Alors of the Sorbonne.

7. The shoes hurt my feet I ought to buy a different pair.

8. Among the items she bought were a sweater, made of yellow and green wool, a jumper, in a soft yellow, and a handbag, also in yellow.

9. Andrew was her best friend when they were children, however, she doesn't get along with him anymore.

10. Dorothy was known as an excellent skater, therefore, it was no surprise when she won a gold medal in the Olympics.

 ## The Colon :

The COLON indicates that the words which follow it will explain more fully what has just been stated.   Primarily, the COLON is used after a *complete* lead-in sentence which announces that a list or an explanation follows.

Example: Her facial expression signified one thing: total interest in what he was saying.

Example: Lee has to choose among several careers: veterinarian, optometrist, and teacher.

Caution: Do not use the colon after an incomplete portion of a sentence unless you are introducing a series of items that appear on separate lines in a list.

Incorrect: Lee has to choose among: veterinarian, optometrist, and teacher as career choices.

Drill 4—Read the following sentences.   Place a colon wherever you think necessary.   The first one is done for you.   There are three sentences that do not require a colon.

1. The celebration included the following activities: a dinner party, a dance, an award, and fireworks.

2. My program this term includes English, algebra, Spanish, and typing.

3. On his trip to New York City, he visited many famous places the United Nations, the World Trade Center, the Empire State Building, the Statue of Liberty, Rockefeller Center, and the Bronx Zoo.

4. When she was in the store, her manner indicated one thing frustration.

5. Our committee included Lucy, Bonnie, Irma, and Ruth.

6. Our club has the following offices President, Vice President, Secretary, and Treasurer.

7. There are four basic directions north, south, east, and west.

8. Sigmund Freud is given an impressive title the Father of Psychiatry.

9. Shakespeare's plays fall into four categories histories, comedies, tragedies, and romances.

10. Shakespeare's plays can be classified as histories, comedies, tragedies, or romances.

Review Exercise   Many of the following sentences contain at least one mistake in punctuation, involving the period, the comma, the semicolon, or the colon. If there is a mistake, the mark may be either left out entirely or incorrectly placed above the letters *a, b, c,* or *d.* When you find a mistake, circle the letter where it occurs. If you find a sentence without any mistake, circle <u>no error</u> at the end of the sentence.
e

Example: The address<u>:</u> which you should make note o<u>f,</u> is 401 Ave
A. no error ⓐ   b   ©
<u>d</u>   e

a is circled because the colon is incorrect; there should be a comma.
c is circled because there is no period after the abbreviation *Ave.*

Example: On our trip through the Southwest, we drove through the
a
following states: Arizona, Texas, and New Mexico. (no error)
b   c   d   e
no error is circuled because all the punctuation is correct.

1. Mr. Hastings, who was our minister, stared at the tired hungry
a   b   c   d
mob that began to gather in front of the church. no error
e

2. Instead of stopping the young woman in the new Corvette stepped
$\overline{}$ **a** $\qquad$ $\overline{}$ **b** $\qquad$ $\overline{}$ **c**

on the gas   no error
$\overline{}$ **d** $\overline{}$ **e**

3. When Bob saw all the soda being served at the party he sug-
$\overline{}$ **a**

gested that he be allowed to serve the big fat, salty pretzels he
$\overline{}$ **b** $\qquad\qquad\qquad$ $\overline{}$ **c** $\qquad$ $\overline{}$ **d**

brought with him.   no error
$\qquad\qquad\qquad\quad$ $\overline{}$ **e**

4. Mr Paretti; who used to be our plumber, has recently, retired.
$\overline{}$ **a** $\quad$ $\overline{}$ **b** $\qquad\qquad\qquad$ $\overline{}$ **c** $\qquad$ $\overline{}$ **d**

no error
$\overline{}$ **e**

5. I am taking algebra, history, science, and English in junior
$\qquad\qquad\qquad\qquad\qquad$ $\overline{}$ **a** $\quad$ $\overline{}$ **b** $\quad$ $\overline{}$ **c**

college.   no error
$\overline{}$ **d** $\overline{}$ **e**

6. J. D. Salinger wrote *The Catcher in the Rye,* which most teenagers
$\overline{}$ **a** $\qquad\qquad$ $\overline{}$ **b** $\quad$ $\overline{}$ **c**

seem to enjoy reading.   no error
$\overline{}$ **d** $\qquad\qquad$ $\overline{}$ **e**

7. In the morning we ate ham and eggs, in the evening we ate beef,
$\qquad\qquad\qquad\qquad$ $\overline{}$ **a** $\quad$ $\overline{}$ **b** $\qquad\qquad\qquad\qquad$ $\overline{}$ **c**

vegetables, and beans.   no error
$\overline{}$ **d** $\qquad\qquad$ $\overline{}$ **e**

8. The price of the car, of course, is determined by the following:
$\qquad\qquad\qquad\qquad$ $\overline{}$ **a** $\qquad\qquad\qquad\qquad\qquad$ $\overline{}$ **b**

size of the engine; extras, such as whitewall tires, radio, and
$\qquad\qquad\qquad\quad$ $\overline{}$ **c**

heater; and prevailing economic conditions.   no error
$\overline{}$ **d** $\qquad\qquad\qquad\qquad\qquad$ $\overline{}$ **e**

9. She had two papers due within two weeks, therefore, she was
$\qquad\qquad\qquad\qquad\qquad\qquad$ $\overline{}$ **a** $\qquad$ $\overline{}$ **b**

quite concerned when the following things happened: her type-
$\qquad\qquad\qquad\qquad\qquad\qquad\qquad$ $\overline{}$ **c**

writer broke, she lost her library card.   no error
$\overline{}$ **d** $\qquad\qquad\qquad$ $\overline{}$ **e**

10. After failing his road test once, Enrico tried to do everything as
$\qquad\qquad\qquad\qquad$ $\overline{}$ **a**

excellently as possible: he made sure to check his rearview mir-
$\qquad\qquad\qquad\qquad\quad$ $\overline{}$ **b**

ror, to fasten his seat belt, and to use hand signals.   no error
$\overline{}$ **c** $\qquad\qquad$ $\overline{}$ **d** $\qquad\qquad\qquad$ $\overline{}$ **e**

Lesson 2
Mechanics

 Capitalization

The use of standard capitalization also helps your reader understand your writing. In this section, we will concentrate on the three major categories for capitalization: proper names, key words in titles, and first words in sentences. Remember to avoid unnecessary capitals.

Proper Names   All proper names should be capitalized.

John **M**ilton, **W**illiam **S**hakespeare, and **E**mily **D**ickinson are well-known poets.

Our home is in **O**ak **P**ark, a suburb of **C**hicago.

Many students say **F**riday is their favorite day because school is over for the week.

People worship **G**od in many different ways.

Words used as important parts of proper names are also capitalized.

I live on **M**ott **A**venue in **F**ar **R**ockaway. (Note that *Avenue* is capitalized.)

We went camping at **L**ake **G**eorge.

The **E**mpire **S**tate **B**uilding is a famous landmark.

Words derived from proper names and most abbreviations are capitalized.

Al is a **N**ew **Y**orker.

We all watch that show on **TV**.

Key Words in Titles   In titles of books, plays, and essays, capital-ize the first word, last word, and other important words. Note: Arti-cles (*a, an, the*), prepositions, and conjunctions are not capitalized unless they begin a title.

> Before it was a movie, *All the President's Men* was a successful book.

> The first Beatles movie was called *A Hard Day's Night.*

> The assignment is to write an essay with the title "**W**hat **I**s **W**rong with **S**chool."

First Word of a Sentence   All sentences must begin with a capital letter.

> **S**he told me not to do it.

> **I**n any event, I am determined to go.

Quoted sentences should also begin with a capital.

> The teacher yelled, "**P**ut that chair down!"

> The student replied, "**I**'m sorry, Mr. Zolkowski."

The three main categories for using capital letters are:

1. proper names
2. key words in titles
3. first word of a sentence

Drill 1—Read the following sentences. Change any letter to a capital if you feel it is necessary.

1. my mother told the telephone repairer, "the phone in that room is broken."
2. "the six million dollar man" is a popular TV series.
3. april is said to be the most beautiful month in england.
4. jimmy carter was inaugurated in washington, d.c.
5. she and i really enjoy mathematics.
6. i wanted to go to college, so i applied to fordham university.

7. *stranger in a strange land* is a science fiction novel very popular with teenagers.

8. gary and i went to our neighborhood high school, bayside high school.

9. when we went to france, we visited notre dame cathedral.

10. dr. martin luther king jr.'s most famous speech included the affirmation, "i have a dream."

M2 The Apostrophe '

As we have pointed out earlier, the APOSTROPHE is used with nouns to indicate possession.

John's hat

The children's milk

The APOSTROPHE is also used to indicate missing letters in a contraction.

Let's go. (*Let's* is a contraction of *let us.*)

Marcella can't come. (*Can't* is a contraction of *cannot.*)

The two main uses of the apostrophe are:

1. to indicate possession
2. to indicate missing letters in a contraction

Drill 2—Read the following sentences. Place an apostrophe, or delete one, wherever necessary.

1. His shoe size and his fathers were the same.
2. "Theyll do it," said my aunt's.
3. The Smith's went over last week to their neighbors house.
4. Emily didn't feel well this afternoon after she drank Toms soda.
5. Janes paper is the only one I havent finished marking yet.

212

6. The doctors office was so crowded that patients had to stand.

7. Myrna and Daniel Jones have a beautiful house; the Jones house cost $75 000.

8. I haven t the time to do my exercise's.

9. Why dont you let your little brother sit in the playgrounds sand-box?

10. Theyre ashamed of their accent although it sounds so lilting.

Review Exercise   Read each of the sentences carefully to see if there is an error in capitalization or mechanics in the spots marked *a, b, c,* and *d.* If there is, circle the letter where the mistake occurs. If there is no error, circle no error.
                                                                        e

1. We lived at 21 Dover Road, Milville, Louisiana, near the Missis-
                      a   b   c
   sippi river.   no error
        d   e

2. I remember the teacher's exact words: "Its important that you
                                           a b
   read Frost's poem 'Mending Wall' for the test."   no error
        c   d   e

3. The teacher spoke to the children's nurses in the park while the
                                      a   b
   principal smiled at the parents wheeling their babies carriages.
   c   d
   no error
        e

4. On January 19, 1809, Edgar Allen Poe was born in Boston, Massa-
      a   b   c   d
   chusetts.   no error
               e

5. Mildred had given Jeanne the money to order the book as a gift;
   a   b
   therefore, Jeanne asked the store to send it to Mildred's mother
                                                       c
   in the South.   no error.
        d   e

6. The essay "How to Be Your Own Best Friend" deals with prob-
             a   b   c
   lems faced by many Teenagers.   no error
                      d   e

7. A salad at a restaurant is a good indication of how edible the food

is; King's Restaurant serves a deliciously fresh salad containing
   a   b c   d
lettuce, carrots, tomatoes, and cucumbers. no error
                                                      e

8. Olga left the USSR in the '60s, and she was lucky to get into the
                              a
USA, to enter one of New York City's universities, and eventually
                              b   c
to graduate with honor's. no error
              d   e

9. Instead of living on a commune in the country, Joe became an
                                         a
accountant in a big city, where he hated the pressure's on him
b   c
and the feeling that he couldn't get out. no error
                    d   e

10. Sam's hair was a nice color but was very frizzy; instead of bat-
       a
tling it continually, he had it cut short; now it curl's naturally
                                                    b
and it's so easy to take care of that he won't have to worry.
        c   d
no error
       e

Lesson 3

Spelling

Throughout this book, you have learned that writing involves two people: you (the writer) and your reader. Misspelled words are distracting and are irritating to a reader. Having to stop and decipher misspelled words prevents your reader from giving full attention to your work. Writing an essay with all words spelled correctly will enable you to communicate with your reader to the best extent possible.

One way to ensure that your essay will contain no spelling errors is to check hard words in the dictionary. Occasionally, a word may be difficult to find. Fortunately, the beginning sound of many words is relatively easy to recognize. Therefore, you should be able to find most hard-to-spell words in the dictionary by using the guide words at the top of the page and by following the principles of alphabetical order.

It is also important that you write or type your paper in neat, legible form. If you are *writing* a final draft, be sure to carefully distinguish each letter. Avoid slanting or crowding your letters together. A clear hand will make a good impression on your reader.

If you are *typing*, leave adequate margins and double space your essay. Whether you are writing or typing your essay, though, it is very important to *proofread* your final draft for hasty misspellings or typographical errors.

Many of you have been forced to learn long, involved spelling rules, which never seemed to help when you needed to spell a troublesome word. You will not find any such rules below. To learn how to spell a word correctly, follow these simple steps:

1. Look at the word closely.

2. Visualize it in your mind.

3. Say it out loud.

4. Write it down carefully.

5. Check the spelling.

Read the list on the following page thoroughly and carefully. Pay special attention to the letter or letters in blue. These are the troublesome parts of the word.

WORDS MOST FREQUENTLY MISSPELLED

absence
accepted
accommodate
achievement
acquire
acquaint
across
all right
analyze
apartment
apology
appreciate
argument
arithmetic
author
awkward

beginning
believe
benefited
brief
business
buying

coming
committee
completely
conscious
consistent
controlled
controversy
correspondence
criticize

decision
definitely
describe
desperate
develop
disease
doesn't

easily
eighth

embarrass
environment
equipment
excellent
exercise
existence
experience
explanation

finally
financial
foreign
forty
fourth

government
grammar

immediately
instructor
intelligent
interest
interfere
interpret

laboratory
leisure
license
library
loneliness

marriage
misspelled
mortgage

necessary
neighbor
ninety
noticeable

occasion
occurred
omitted
opportunity

particular
pastime
performance

physician
pleasant
poison
possess
precede
preferred
prejudice
privilege
probably
professor
psychology

receive
recommend
reference
religion
restaurant
rhythm
running

secretary
separate
similar
sincerely
studying
succeed
success
surprise

thorough
toward
tragedy
tries
truly

unnecessary
until
using

various
village
villain

Wednesday
writing
written

Drill 1—Following the five steps on page 215, go through every word on the list. If you did not spell the word correctly when you wrote it down, begin again with the first step.

Drill 2—Select the 10 words on this list with which you had the most difficulty. Look these words up in a dictionary and write down their meanings.

1. _____
2. _____
3. _____
4. _____
5. _____
6. _____
7. _____
8. _____
9. _____
10. _____

Drill 3—Using the 10 words you defined, write one sentence for each word.

1. _____
2. _____
3. _____
4. _____
5. _____
6. _____
7. _____
8. _____
9. _____
10. _____

Review Exercise 1   In each of the groups of words below, one word is misspelled. Note the misspelled word, and decide how to correct it by indicating on your answer sheet one of the following:

a. Switch letters around—for example, change *ie* to *ei*.

b. Take out one letter.

c. Put in one letter.

d. Change one letter to another—for example, change *e* to *i* or *r* to *a*.

Example:
    writting is the misspelled word. Since you correct the error by taking out one letter (choice *b*), your answer would be (b) *writing*.

1. acquaint
all right
desease
believe

2. business
begining
decision
interest

3. definitely
discribe
experience
toward

4. Wednesday
sincerly
exercise
similar

5. succeed
government
preformance
writing

6. precede
pastime
professor
recomend

7. ninety
immediately
existance
arithmetic

8. studying
opportunity
writen
develop

9. license
recieve
religion
village

10. villain
controlled
arguement
possess

11. achievement
secretary
poisin
reference

12. psychology
enviroment
easily
equipment

13. eighth
grammer
rhythm
fourth

14. criticize
akward
apartment
success

15. completely
    occasion
    privelege
    various

16. excellent
    accepted
    runing
    consistent

17. appreciate
    misspelled
    liesure
    loneliness

18. foreign
    surprise
    prefered
    explanation

19. interpret
    thorough
    neighbor
    noticable

20. truly
    interfere
    mariage
    prejudice

21. instructor
    acquire
    coming
    commitee

22. analyze
    necessary
    tragady
    conscious

23. physician
    pleasant
    accomodate
    finally

24. tries
    particular
    embaras
    buying

25. breif
    unnecessary
    using
    until

26. author
    apology
    fourty
    probably

27. benefited
    omited
    correspondence
    doesn't

28. laboratory
    desparate
    mortgage
    across

29. abcence
    financial
    separate
    intelligent

30. library
    occurred
    resturant
    controversy

Guide to Revising Papers

INDEX

A

C

E

F

G

I

K

L

M

N

O

P

S

Secondary elements of the sentence, 155, 163

Semicolon, 142, 206
  to separate coordinate elements in series, 142, 206
  to separate independent clauses, 142, 206

Sentence:
  complex, 154, 172, 175
  compound, 154, 173–175
  defined, 155
  fragment, 136–137, 155, 181–182
  run-together, 143–144, 155, 185–186
  simple, 155, 170–171, 175

Simple sentence, 155, 170–171, 175

Simple subject, 156

Spelling, 144, 215–219

Subject (of essay):
  finding one, 49–50, 52–53
  limiting it, 54–56, 58–60

Subject:
  agreement with verb (*see* Agreement of subject-verb)
  complement, 161
  compound, 170
  simple, 156

Subordinating conjunctions, 165, 172

Supporting-detail sentence:
  defined, 3, 23
  types of supporting-detail sentences, 27–28, 37

Supporting-details, 23, 37

T

Tense, 146

2 3 4 5 6 7 8 9 10 VHVH 87 86 85 84 83 82 81 80 79